Gardening for Children with Autism Spectrum Disorders and Special Educational Needs

of related interest

Playing, Laughing and Learning with Children on the Autism Spectrum
A Practical Resource of Play Ideas for Parents and Carers
2nd Edition
Julia Moor
ISBN 978 1 84310 608 1
eISBN 978 1 84642 824 1

Get Out, Explore, and Have Fun!
How Families of Children with Autism or Asperger Syndrome Can Get the Most out of Community Activities
Lisa Jo Rudy
ISBN 978 1 84905 809 4
eISBN 978 0 85700 385 0

Motivate to Communicate!
300 Games and Activities for Your Child with Autism
Simone Griffin and Dianne Sandler
ISBN 978 1 84905 041 8
eISBN 978 0 85700 215 0

Fun with Messy Play
Ideas and Activities for Children with Special Needs
Tracey Beckerleg
ISBN 978 1 84310 641 8
eISBN 978 1 84642 854 8

Multisensory Rooms and Environments
Controlled Sensory Experiences for People with Profound and Multiple Disabilities
Susan Fowler
Foreword by Paul Pagliano
ISBN 978 1 84310 462 9
eISBN 978 1 84642 809 8

Practical Sensory Programmes
For Students with Autism Spectrum Disorder and Other Special Needs
Sue Larkey
ISBN 978 1 84310 479 7
eISBN 978 1 84642 567 7

Natasha Etherington

Gardening for Children with Autism Spectrum Disorders and Special Educational Needs

Engaging with Nature to Combat
Anxiety, Promote Sensory Integration
and Build Social Skills

Jessica Kingsley *Publishers*
London and Philadelphia

Disclaimer
Any plant substance has the potential to cause an allergic reaction in some people, so use due caution.
Not all plants and animals mentioned in this book will be found in the UK.

The epigraph on p.9 is reproduced with kind permission from Richard Louv.
The photograph on p.100 is reproduced with kind permission from Lee Valley Tools Ltd.
Drawing on p.105 reproduced with kind permission from Dolores Altin.
Extract from AHTA Position Paper 2007 on pp.136–138 is reproduced with kind permission from the American Horticultural Therapy Association.

First published in 2012
by Jessica Kingsley Publishers
116 Pentonville Road
London N1 9JB, UK
and
400 Market Street, Suite 400
Philadelphia, PA 19106, USA

www.jkp.com

Library of Congress Cataloging in Publication Data
Etherington, Natasha.
   Gardening for children with autism spectrum disorders and special educational needs : engaging with nature to combat anxiety, promote sensory integration and build social skills / Natasha Etherington.
      p. cm.
   ISBN 978-1-84905-278-8 (alk. paper)
   1. Autism in children--Treatment. 2. Children with autism spectrum disorders. 3. Gardening--Therapeutic use. 4. Gardening for children. 5. Behavior therapy--Methods. I. Title.
   RJ506.A9E84 2012
   618.92'85882--dc23
                                        2011032909

British Library Cataloguing in Publication Data
A CIP catalogue record for this book is available from the British Library

ISBN 978 1 84905 278 8
eISBN 978 0 85700 599 1

Printed and bound in Great Britain

For Karen Rosemary Lewis
11 September 1942 – 5 November 2008

Acknowledgements

Sincere thanks to Jessica Kingsley, publisher, Emily McClave, commissioning editor, Victoria Peters, production editor, and Christine Firth, copy editor.

With thanks to Jason.

Contents

Chapter 1

Introduction

The garden needs to be part of the new nature movement.

Richard Louv, author of The Nature Principle, speaking at EPIC Sustainable Living Expo, 14 May 2011, Vancouver

I love to be outside, to get wet, dig and grow plants. It makes me feel alive and connected to Mother Earth. Having worked with special needs youth as a horticultural therapist, I was inspired to write this book for teachers, school counsellors, support assistants, parents, and anybody else interested in this subject, regardless of their horticultural know-how. Support teachers are faced with the day to day challenges of engaging students with special needs within the education system. In my work I see how motivational gardening is. This book will show you how a horticultural therapy programme will fill a void that isn't accessible to a special needs student within a classroom. I also hope to improve the mental health of teachers, carers and parents by getting you outside enjoying the benefits of nature.

For parents I hope these activities will show you a different side to your child, build some fond memories and experiences and show you how working in different environments can help increase positive behaviours.

Key is the significance of the people–plant relationship. Horticultural therapists understand the power of plants. Plants purify our air and supply our food. Plants meet our demands by providing nourishment to all our senses whether invigorating us or calming our minds. Plants offer pure aesthetic pleasure and some plants go even further to heal and restore our bodies. Whether you like it or not, we cannot exist without plants, but with us or not they will still exist.

I have written this book keeping ease of reference in mind, and I have added useful information such as how to carry out a risk assessment as an appendix for quick access (see Appendix 2). Please read the Introduction, Chapter 2 on 'Mindfulness Approach', and Chapter 3 on 'Why Dig?' Each of the subsequent chapters outlines the benefits of gardening in relation to a special need or condition. Therefore, I would recommend that for attention deficit hyperactivity disorder, for example, which often occurs with coexisting conditions of anxiety, depression, sensory impairments and learning disabilities, that you also read Chapters 5 and 7, and try Activities 3 and 4 in Chapter 8.

What is horticultural therapy?

Horticultural therapy is the engagement of a person in gardening related activities, facilitated by a trained therapist, to achieve specific treatment goals. First and foremost the goal is the reduction of negative arousal levels, which leads to improved health, allowing a number of positive changes to take place. In horticultural therapy, plants, gardens and natural landscapes are utilized to engage and improve cognitive, physical, social, emotional and spiritual well-being by parents, support staff or trained therapists. It may be passive or active.

Why is horticultural therapy important?

Horticultural therapy is important for all the following reasons:

- Any nature setting or garden has a wealth of tools of engagement available.

- Through nurturing plants we make learning more meaningful.

- Cognitive development, psychological growth, social skill learning and prevocational work skills can all be developed in a garden setting.

- A garden is a safe and familiar environment to us.

- We understand the age old ritual of giving and receiving plants.

- Before headache pills and antibiotics, we looked to medicinal herbs and plants to cure us.

- Getting outside reduces anxiety and depression.

- Exercise is important for our brains and mood; it helps to create new synapses.

- Plants provide sensory stimulation, flowers and leaves for drying and arrangements, and herbs for cooking and crafts.

For additional benefits and related research, please see the American Horticultural Therapy Association (AHTA) position paper in Appendix 3.

Chapter 2

Mindfulness Approach

> The secret of health for both mind and body is not to mourn for the past, worry about the future, or anticipate troubles, but to live in the present moment wisely and earnestly.
>
> *Buddha*

The mindfulness approach is a non-spiritual approach adapted from Buddhism which I have embraced in my day to day personal life and work as a horticultural therapist. The essence of mindfulness is awareness of mind and body through regular meditation. Through meditation we can enjoy a garden passively and learn through the approach of loving kindness and compassion to all beings. This book is not about meditation; however, I believe that it is easier to enable individuals to actively experience and understand the people–plant relationship through the mindfulness approach as follows.

Introducing the mindfulness approach to young people with special needs

Introducing the concept of the people–plant relationship involves recognizing that interconnectiveness is a fundamental principle of nature and a source of great comfort to many people. It is important to appreciate the 'being' mode as opposed to the 'doing' mode. In the 'doing' mode we are not aware of our present emotions and thoughts, rushing around not thinking before we speak. In the 'being' mode a person is able to stop, consider and examine their present emotions and thoughts. The result is greater compassion and patience. Once a person gains patience they are able to see situations with a fresh mind and less anxiety.

Through regular participation in the garden, we can set tasks that require effort and lead to increased self-awareness. The mindfulness approach gives children and young people the opportunity to:

- use a compassionate non-judgemental approach (considering what you think and how you see things before acting)
- be open to experience as it occurs
- remain adaptable and flexible to the moment
- be patient and encourage the practice of curiosity in our relationship with Mother Earth
- understand that in life there is joy and sorrow which in turn teaches resilience
- become aware of seeds of negativity in our minds
- accept that we cannot control everything that happens in life
- understand actions and consequences.

I find that children are naturally quite mindful; however, they are usually far too busy to observe their successes or achievements. As carers or teachers we can help them find greater awareness in their strengths through mindfully noting their successes while gardening alongside them. For example, a child digging for some time in the digging plot thoroughly engrossed in finding worms and tree roots does not realize, until you point it out, that they have great focus and a positive personal strength of perseverance.

Teaching a child to focus on the present moment will help with learning not to interrupt. Other benefits include teaching the child to learn to think before speaking, to ask politely for equipment and tools, and to consider other people's emotions. For example, if your friend's plant gets eaten overnight by slugs, will you share your plant with them or give your plant to them? How will you work together to make sure the same thing doesn't happen to your plant tonight? There is nothing quite like waiting for a plant to grow to teach us that most esteemed trait of patience.

The simplest method to introduce the concept of mindfulness to your child is to go outside and either sit or stand very still. This is the first step in training the child's attention to focus on what is relevant and to train the child to focus on what we are learning without being distracted. An ability to focus is critical for learning in school and for maintaining friendships. If it's raining, take off your hat, lower your umbrella and feel the rain on your face. Taste it. Observe how your body feels. Is it pleasant or unpleasant? If the sun is out, feel the sun warm your face, body and heart. Imagine you are a bee warming your wings in the sun ready to fly. You are re-energizing and going to be a busy bee gardening just as the bee is going to pollinate your plants and collect nectar. You are in 'being' mode, which means you are experiencing the present moment and in the flow.

How plants can help us relate to children's concerns

As parents and teachers it is useful to accept that we see life differently to children. By appreciating this need and taking steps to understand their viewpoint we can have greater empathy for any concerns children may have regarding:

- illness and adjusting to disability
- using medication

- puberty

- sexual reproduction.

Gardeners understand that plants grow in their own time and way. Some prefer shade, others full sun and some like a little of both. As we work with plants we learn which plants work best where. In Chapter 5 I discuss in greater detail how using plant analogies can help children understand issues such as taking medication, growth patterns and sexual reproduction. Children will learn that when a plant does not fulfil expectations it's OK to feel disappointed. Using the activities in this book can help you gain an understanding of what your child wants and needs. You may be surprised to learn that your child's favourite activity is weeding or sweeping the floor. Ask yourself what it is about this activity that they enjoy so much? Something so simple yet so satisfying... This is perhaps an activity they feel in control of, that they have mastered and feel they do very well.

Through working together in the garden you will gain a greater acceptance of who your child is. For example, when we sow seeds we gain a sense of anticipation as we watch and wait to see seedlings grow. Over time we may come to realize that even though we may have given those seeds the best conditions to germinate, for some reason beyond our control (e.g. adverse weather), some seeds will not germinate.

An example I use for children to understand acceptance is that we are all unique flowers. We will open in our own unique way and in our own particular cycle. This can be of great reassurance to many children with developmental delays.

The first step you can take to understand a child's point of view is to listen. Give them time to talk, then find opportunities for them to excel and gain mastery of an activity. At at all times use compassion. I've built dead snowmen, seen children say and do some very odd stuff but this is just them being a child and so we should not judge them as an adult. This includes not using labels to describe a child but looking at them as an individual.

Finally, do not take every action a child does too seriously (unless of course it is dangerous). Try not to get fixated on one particular bad behaviour. Use distraction as a means to finish the activity and then discuss with colleagues and parents how to work on this particular behaviour rather than letting it make you angry, which is a negative state of mind.

How mindfulness and flow work

When we are absorbed in an activity such as weeding or sowing seeds, we calm our minds and start subconsciously to analyse our experiences in life. When we smell a fragrant rose or taste a herb like mint, we are connecting with the present moment. Becoming immersed in a moment we are stimulating our senses. Observe your senses, sight, sound, smell, taste and touch. By purposefully connecting with our senses we naturally calm our minds a little. When we're in the 'flow' (Sikszentmihalyi 1990; Getzels and Csikszentmihalyi 1976) we feel at one with the world, more able to let go of worries and problems as we're not completely focused on our worries but more on the task in hand; we're satisfied and happy. Through this process we gain a greater sense of ourselves and may realize an obstacle or negative influence that until this moment we had denied. With renewed strength and energy, we should be able to take the next step in trying to figure out a solution which is a positive state of mind. An environment for greater self-awareness is the overall goal.

Mindfulness helps us realize that the past, present and future are all interwoven. I believe this knowledge helps to reduce feelings of hopelessness commonly experienced by children and young people with special needs.

Chapter 3

Why Dig?

Digging is a primeval and familiar task to us all. Give students the time to play and explore in the soil: it's in the soil that our relationship with Mother Earth begins. It is essential that you identify an area that can become a digging plot. Perhaps you have a raised bed already built that can be used by the special needs programme. It may even be a large container of soil. Children with special needs deserve their own designated area in which they can feel comfortable and not worry about upsetting anyone. Put a sign up over the digging plot stating 'Digging welcome' and leave a covered container of hand trowels nearby. It's by playing in the soil, digging up tree roots and discovering stones and worms that children's curiosities are captured. They will never forget the smell of soil. In the digging plot they will form a long lasting relationship with the earth. It won't be long before they're demanding to plant and learn more. Now you've created the interest, you've got the perfect learning environment.

Some examples of making connections

Making connections involves physical elements, emotional elements and being outside.

PHYSICAL ELEMENTS

Gardening is an age-appropriate activity which incorporates play and gross motor skills. Through gardening, children will learn positive associations with exercise while reducing muscle tension and lowering blood pressure. Children are using endurance and dexterity to dig. While they are gardening, speech is encouraged to share discoveries and cooperate with buddies.

EMOTIONAL ELEMENTS

There are essentially three sorts of feelings: pleasant, unpleasant and neutral. Through digging we can identify and be in touch with our feelings as they come and go. Digging is a good activity for children with aggressive tendencies, agitation and mood swings. It will tire them out and allow them to take out their frustrations on the earth. Children who have anxieties, feelings of inadequacy, inability to cope and hopelessness will quickly be motivated and their negative feelings will lessen as they dig.

Gardening is an easily achievable activity which can be experienced whatever the barrier, be it a wheelchair, sensory sensitivity or visual impairment. Digging requires some effort but should not be a struggle. If a child is struggling, you need to consider how you can adapt this activity to the particular child's needs, or you may need to work side by side in the digging plot rather than supervising from the sidelines.

Familiarity with a nature setting makes us feel safe. We feel a sense of accomplishment when we remove a large tree root: we've been digging all week and we've learned perseverance. Also we will understand more about ourselves and our friends. We can have fun with our friends in the digging plot, and feel free and happy. We can get messy without getting into trouble. We will get tired out. How will we deal with fatigue? Are we willing to explore and try new activities?

Through stimulating our senses we're becoming more aware of our own bodies and connecting emotions and feelings. If we experience a feeling which is not unpleasant or pleasant, we can be aware that we are experiencing a 'neutral feeling'. Through all this effort of digging we calm our body, which helps to calm our minds in the present moment.

BEING OUTSIDE

We all feel a sense of relief when we get outside. Before going outside, create a sense of anticipation and curiosity. Ask the children: What will we find in the digging plot today? What is going on in the garden today? Is it raining, wet or windy? I wonder if the bird feeder needs more seeds? Get wet, get a little cold and feel alive.

Social interaction and communication

There is much in the digging plot to be discovered. These discoveries can be shared with peers and also presented to the teacher and class. Children will learn to follow verbal directions and safety precautions. This activity encourages judgement and independent thinking. Consider hiding small toys in the digging plot to reward motivation and entice reluctant children to the digging plot.

Teach the correct names of tools to be used and ask children to teach their peers these. If working one to one with a child in the garden, encourage a buddy to come out and work with them. This child will become popular very quickly as a digging plot is every child's dream come true. Maths test or digging plot? It's not a hard sell.

Encourage children to cooperate together, for instance by only having one hand trowel to work with. Encourage sharing and awareness of others' needs and feelings. If a child is experiencing an unpleasant feeling, ask the child to share it, describe it and examine how long it lasts.

Often, through naming the feeling and through breathing exercises (see Appendix 6) we can overcome our fears of unpleasant experiences and actually reverse the negative associations such as the racing heartbeat (panic attack) to a positive one of digging in the plot with our new friends in the present moment.

Some interesting facts about soil

The facts below could help you to engage your students:

- The earth's soil has been formed over millions of years. Soil is not made overnight!

- There are four basic components to soil: organic materials, inorganic materials, air and water.

- Organic materials include decomposed insects and other invertebrates, as well as decaying plant material.

- It's not dirt, it's soil! Try to use the correct term. We respect the word 'soil'. Children with tactile sensitivities don't seem quite as worried about soil as they do with the term 'dirt'.

- The largest portion of the soil is non-living, or inorganic matter. Inorganic materials are sand, silt and clay. These are formed by the wind and rain wearing down rocks. Soil is the term we use to describe the surface layer of the earth. Of course, this varies from place to place such as a desert, forest or agricultural site.

- Roots from plants dig deep into the soil, creating passages for water and air. Invertebrates such as worms, snakes, and small mammals such as mice and rats all till the earth.

- Soil is biologically active, which means it is home to thousands of micro-organisms, invertebrates and plant roots.

- 'Bio' means 'life'.
- There are between 20 million and 2 billion bacteria per teaspoon of soil.
- There are many different types of soil, including sandy, clay and loam.
- Plants have preferences for certain types of soil and weather conditions.
- Soil has a pH value, which means it may be acidic, neutral or alkaline (a bit like our feelings!).
- Soil colour can vary dramatically, for example soil that has dried out (light grey) compared to fresh soil taken from the earth (deep brown).

For more facts on soil check out the Soil Foodweb Canada Website (www.soilfoodweb.ca).

Safety tips

When digging (unless you have a very large space) don't allow a group of students to use spades or shovels as it is too easy for someone to get hit. Use hand trowels instead. In winter and early spring, check the earth isn't too frozen as tools will slip and could cut a student.

I recommend a risk assessment of your garden or nature setting. See the example of a risk assessment in Appendix 2. Before beginning gardening, arrive five minutes early to take a look around the garden, clearing away safety hazards such as electric leads or cables that might trip a student up or other distractions like balls.

Always tidy up the tools after digging. I leave a container of sand (with a cup or two of vegetable oil mixed in) for hand trowels to be left in and for easy cleaning.

Chapter 4

Autism Spectrum Disorder

Approach

The main goal for the horticultural therapist is to teach skills using a developmental social pragmatic model as an approach. This focuses on initiation and spontaneity in communication following the child's focus of attention and motivations in a natural environment. The joy of gardening is that these skills are taught in context. According to experts in the autism spectrum disorder (ASD) field, it is critically important to teach older ASD learners social skills in context. The garden becomes your outdoor sensory classroom to teach life skills.

Engaging with a child in a garden or nature setting will help the child learn positive social patterns and provide the skills to see how the world works (skills transferable to other settings, such as gripping and opening or managing behaviours) while gaining mastery of activities, which leads to improved self-esteem.

Once while walking a child from the classroom to the garden I was asked if I was the video game replacement and I was happy to be the replacement. I strongly believe in the good of getting children with ASD outside and encouraged to garden. Yes, you may hear the support team saying that the child is becoming fixated or obsessive with the garden. This is not a problem. I believe that this is a good thing and far better to be fixated on nature, eating carrots and exercising than being stuck indoors playing on a video game and snacking on chips.

I understand any apprehension you may initially have about entering a garden setting but I urge you to embrace whatever risks you perceive and to have a go as often as you feel you can fit it into a child's schedule. Repetition is key. There is a lot we can do to be ready for a visit to the garden and I hope this book will allay your concerns.

Note to parents

Getting outside with your children will help you assess their nervous system: hearing, seeing, touching, smelling and moving. This takes regular commitment all through the year. Encourage all your children to work together in the garden. Ask siblings to respond positively to the find presented to them. It may be a worm, a piece of glass or a lumpy stone. They may have to act a little bit but this shared interaction is deeply enriching for all ASD learners. If this is not possible, try to arrange a play date and ask the parent of the other child whether you could make this a regular 'nature play date'. If social interaction isn't a key worry you have right now, it will be in the future. These play dates are important in helping to build social skills for more complex situations later on in life.

Note to teachers

Nature play for ASD learners is exciting and I hope you will make it a regular part of your students' schedule as a highly motivational learning tool. Be mindful of the present season, and initiate activities that are in tune with the cycle of the seasons. For example, only water the plants on dry days, not on wet days, and top up the bird feeders according to the seasons (use a good nutritional bird seed in winter, and softened fruit, crushed unsalted peanuts and oats in summer; check out birding websites for more information, such as the Royal Society for the Protection of Birds at www.rspb.org.uk and Audubon in North America at www.audubon.org). Through repetition, an understanding will be gained of nature's life cycles and greater sensory awareness will grow. You will therefore need to go outside all through the year. Be prepared and bring some hats along for everyone to wear. Walk in the rain and feel the cold and wet (fold your umbrella up for a little bit).

If you are working with a very agitated child, go for a walk around the school a few times. Not only are you providing a much needed outlet for some potentially aggressive behaviour but also you are setting positive associations with getting outside and exercising. Set the ground rules first. If we go for a walk, we can then go in the garden. Going to the garden is the end goal but if you're working with a student who is way too agitated they're not going to enjoy the opportunity and you're going to get frustrated very quickly. Walking around the school will give both you and the student the opportunity to reset and calm down. Be mindful of the energy state of your students and try to let go of any concerns you may have on getting outside (maybe you have some new shoes on) and concentrate on the present moment.

Observe the students. Look for emotional expression. Are they smiling? Has their breathing quickened? Are they noticing the puddles on the floor or the broken branches or leaves strewn around the school? Encourage them to touch trees, hold twigs, and as a real motivator, let them take home their finds. Are they aware of the weather? If it's raining we won't need to water the garden today. Make a note of what the students find stimulating and exciting. By the way, how are *you* feeling? More alive? Calmer? Maybe you'll run out of time to actually garden that day. That's just fine. Try to remember the next day to ask your students what they did with their finds. Send a note home for their parents to ask them about that twig in their bag. This is strengthening the learning at home and will also give the parents an insight into what is a motivator for their child. The following skills can be learned in the garden setting:

- practising social interaction and life skills

- increasing language skills

- promoting functional communication (making requests and joint attention)

- enhancing self-esteem

- using sensory skills (tactile, visual, oral, aural, taste) in addition to the two internal senses of movement and body awareness

- reducing tactile defensiveness

- having opportunities for symbolic play

- experiencing physical education

- employing flexible thinking and making predictions

- learning collaboration skills

- gaining knowledge of tools, garden plants, the environment and wildlife kingdom

- practising working safely

- using creativity and innovation

- learning about nutrition and the enjoyment of cooking with fresh produce

- going on field trips to garden centres and botanical gardens

- learning about world cultures, plants and gardens

- practising documentation skills by creating a garden journal, scrapbook pictures and plants of interest.

Before starting

Here are some practical guidelines to help you get started:

- All nature play can be structured with a therapeutic purpose. At the heart of the activity should be the function. Try to mix up easy and hard tasks in the activity. Of course, you may be restricted by time so you might want to build up to harder tasks as the children become more familiar with the garden.

- Repetitive activities such as digging provide an outlet for aggressive behaviour and are also great fun.

- Anticipate what might be a distraction and remove from the garden setting items such as balls and skipping ropes.

- All sharp tools, toxic plants (see poisonous plants listed in Chapter 9) and materials should be removed.

- Use every possible opportunity you can to use descriptive words (adjectives), to count and to identify objects and plants.

- Do not expect too much too soon. Through repetition and gardening in context you will succeed.

- Focus on one area such as naming tools and creating a safe, calm and enjoyable environment for the ASD learner so they look forward to the next time.

For children with ASD physical prompting, such as placing your hand on top of their hand to guide a task, will help reduce frustrations. I do this to save numerous lady bugs from being squashed and to lower shovels that have come a bit too close to my face. I will also physically block the pathway or part of a garden I do not want a child to enter. Always provide a social reward such as 'Great work'. This is motivating in itself and promotes the opportunity for more spontaneous verbal behaviour. Don't expect students to be particularly interested in waiting for a plant to grow. They will want to plant it, take it home or move it around. Delayed gratification is too high an expectation for an ASD learner.

Consider bringing in pets such as rabbits or chickens to run and hop around the garden. Don't worry if no gardening gets done that day. Cuddling a rabbit or holding a chicken can be a child's dream come true.

If you are a teacher, always ask for feedback from parents and other carers to find out if the child is improving or talks about gardening at home. Remain flexible like a tree bending in the wind.

Sensory sensitivities

Children on the autism spectrum are especially sensitive to sensory conditions such as sound, lights, touch and taste. A classroom is full of some rather smelly and loud children with for the most part fluorescent lighting overhead. This is not a conducive environment for an ASD learner. You can see how relaxing and calming getting outside for a break from this sensory onslaught into some fresh air might be. Consider having some scented plants in the garden to introduce gradually to the child. They may instinctively try to smell the flower, but may just look at it or hold it, in which case you could suggest they smell it. Always forewarn them that there is a smell. Scents such as roses, lavender and sweet pea are calming. Invigorating smells include mints, citrus fruits and onions.

Some very sensitive children may find very bright flowers such as orange and red ones stressful. Yellow, which is a good colour for visually impaired children, has also been found to be stress inducing. If this is the case for your child I would recommend that you prepare them. Through seasonal visits to the garden you are introducing a child and instilling anticipation for those bright flower blooms. Why not start in the springtime? The garden will be a lush green landscape. Through regular visits to the garden throughout the year any potentially stress inducing flowers that may have been a concern to a child with high sensory sensitivities will be less of a shock to the system as they will be prepared for the flowers to bloom. Regular visits to the digging plot will soon overcome any sensitivity over soil and dirt.

Offer as wide a variety of edible plants as possible in your activities. Herbs are a good addition to any garden and through trying a variety of edible plants you can transfer your horticultural skills into life skills by cooking with your harvest in the kitchen. You'll also learn more about which smells stimulate the child and which repel them and the foods they like to eat and cook (important life skills). Plant herbs or vegetables you know how to cook with. Incorporate harvesting from the garden into your cooking schedules. The smell of a pumpkin or apple pie baking in the oven is unforgettable. You can also dry herbs in the autumn for winter activities.

Some examples of sensory nature play are digging, climbing trees, rolling on lawns and swinging on branches. In the digging plot encourage tactile exploration in the soil such as finding tree roots, worms and stones. Planting and sowing seeds calls for more fine motor skills. Consider using a spoon or small hand tool to pick seeds or weeds with but try to fade the use of tools and encourage just using hands. Use a finger or toes to play in sand if you're working up to using soil. Encourage place fingers or toes into water. Write on stones or pebbles and placing them in a pot of water or a fountain. This can be an insightful activity into the emotions of a student at that moment in time. An agitated child can be distracted by natural sounds such as water running or bird song. Enhance these distractions and adapt them by playing a listening game to identify noises. Listen to sounds that promote calmness. For example, a fountain (however small) with the sound of running water is one of the most calming nature sounds we can experience. I have played CDs of bird song, but I found this annoyed the children more than focused them. There is no replacement for the spontaneous bird song from a small bird's visit to a bird feeder.

Activities

You should work alongside the student in these activities until you feel it is appropriate to introduce a buddy student to work with, at which point you can take a step back. By experiencing what the student is experiencing you may pick up on parts of their personality you hadn't noticed before. You will have many volunteers for these activities.

Please begin with Activity 1, 'Digging', as it's through working in the earth that our curiosity is triggered to learn more about our environment.

Activity 1: Digging

Digging welcome!

Aim

Introducing the child to the garden and to soil; getting to know a child and assessing a child's sensory limitations at that time.

Tools

You will need the following items:

- shovel or hand trowel

- digging plot or container of soil.

If working in soil is not possible, use a container or a sand pit.

The activity

Lead your young learner outside and tell them you have a new digging plot. Pass them a shovel. If you have worries about aggressive tendencies, use a garden hand trowel instead and never turn your back on the student. If you have a very agitated student, starting off your day digging is a very important physical activity that will help redirect aggressive behaviour and help lower anxiety and reset their mood.

Ensure you use the correct name of the tool, not what Grandpa used to call it. You are not going to do anything else today, just dig. Dig together, use this moment to get some exercise and learn about the soil in your garden. Is it a sandy or clay soil? Try to be non-judgemental while digging. If the child decides to lie down in the soil and taste or smell it, please don't say 'No'. You may think their behaviour is really silly but this is all part of learning through play and children with special needs merit time to mess about just the same as their peers. Through digging and exploring in soil, your child will form a relationship with the earth. If working in the soil is not possible at first, try working with sand and build up to soil. Maybe you could dig in the soil nearby and try to entice the child to work with you. Now, let the child lead the digging activity. Follow their lead. Please present real value (with a little bit of acting on your part) to their spontaneous finds be it a worm or a stone. Encourage your child to show their finds to their fellow siblings or class mates and teacher. Perhaps you could prime their teacher beforehand that you may be coming inside to show them a find in the garden and you would appreciate them reacting positively to this. This shared experience is a real self-esteem builder and is setting a basic social interaction skill of sharing. It may also be enlightening for teachers to see what motivates ASD learners.

Always start your day with the digging plot. This routine repetition is so important to children with ASD. Try not to use not digging as a way to reprimand the child. Simply use not gardening as the reprimand. I find it very important as a motivator for working on shifting attention between activities that the child always knows they will be allowed back to the digging plot.

Allow the digging activity to happen regularly before you try to switch activities. If you're just getting outside once a week it may take a month before you switch activities. Ideally you would try to get outside every day, in which case you might feel the child will be ready within a week but either way, don't rush things. This may be boring for you but building an important bridge to nature for your child.

Why not take this opportunity to sing a song such as 'This is the way we dig the soil…' to the tune of the old nursery rhyme 'This is the way we wash our face'. If you do not know this nursery rhyme you can listen to it being sung at www.nurseryrhymes4u.com/NURSERY_RHYMES/Page_930.html.

Soon your child will ask to plant or sow seeds. At this point shift your activity, grab a plant or the nearest seed catalogue and look together at what plants you would like to grow. Now they're hooked!

Activity 2: Trading tools

Aim

Promoting functional communication in making requests, learning to shift attention between activities and share interests and experiences, and increasing cognitive development in learning new tools and processes.

Tools

You will need the following items:

- garden shovel
- fork
- rake
- hand trowel.

The activity

Trading tools is a very useful learning mechanism in increasing cognitive development. By learning tool names we are increasing our vocabulary, being forced to use communication skills and receiving immediate gratification in getting the tool we wanted, all in context. In this activity you will be able to work on shifting attention between tasks. Only start this activity once you feel the child has spent enough time in the digging plot or sand pit. Focus on the digging activity for at least a few weeks. You are building a relationship with the child so that they will learn to trust they will always get some time in the digging plot. You should not aim to do both digging and trading tools until you think the child is ready, and certainly not on the first visit to the garden. This is something that will happen over time.

Remaining flexible and patient is imperative. Which means, of course, if they're asking for the shovel, the project you had planned with your rake or fork may have to wait until another trade is an option.

This activity is also a means to use obstruction (briefly interrupting an activity in a playful way) and sabotage techniques (leaving out a required item needed for an activity) to disrupt the routine of digging. By making the shovel an inaccessible item (the child will need help to access an out-of-reach item) we are forced to communicate and to cooperate politely. Once they have found the tool needed, allow them to take turns and trade tools. This may be quite frustrating for you at times but again, it is an important learning tool. If possible try to find a peer for your child to work with on trading and finding the correct tools. I find most children do not know the correct names for gardening tools. Here you have the perfect opportunity to build self-esteem. The ASD learner can teach their peers the names of these tools.

Activity 3: Identifying parts of a plant

Aim

Introducing basic botany. Learning to identify plant parts. Connecting with what we see and learning to classify plants. This activity should be repeated regularly.

Tools

You will need the following items:

- a non-poisonous plant, such as a dandelion (you do not need to purchase a plant)
- piece of paper and coloured felt-tip pens
- piece of paper on which you have already drawn a plant, with roots, stem and flower for demonstration.

The activity

1. Lead your ASD learner outside and ask them to pull up from the soil the plant you have identified to use in this activity.

2. Ask them if they know what the plant is (do they use the word 'plant'?). Reward them by saying, 'Well done'.

3. Ask the ASD learner to hold the plant. As they feel the parts of the plant name them: roots, stem, flower.

4. Show the student your example drawing. Then remove it and replace it with the plant. Ask them to draw the parts of the plant. You will have to be flexible and adapt to each ASD learner. If this does not work, you may find cutting out parts of a plant from paper and sticking them on another sheet easier and a more

familiar activity to the student. Try with a real plant next time.

This is a multisensory activity which helps us to connect with what we see. Whenever you come across tree roots while digging or planting, remember to point them out. Create situations where you need help naming plant parts. I purposefully forget the names of plant parts. Forgetting the name on your part creates a motivation on the student's part to impress you with what they have learnt and subsequently builds confidence.

Activity 4: Planting

Aim
Promoting flexible thinking and making predictions by introducing planting and learning sequences.

Tools
You will need the following items:

- seeds or plant (whichever you are working with): consider purchasing large seeds such as sunflower or pumpkin seeds. Don't buy flimsy plants – consider sturdy evergreens such as heathers or ornamental grasses (even if held too tight, these plants will regain posture without too much effort)

- plant pot (or as an alternative you could use a yoghurt pot, olive oil can, bucket, coffee container): always punch or drill holes in bottom for drainage

- potting soil (available from any garden centre and some supermarkets)

- water and watering can or bottle

- vermiculite (optional).

The activity
When planting, there is a set sequence:

1. Take a plant pot.

2. Add some soil to the pot.

3. Place the plant in the soil in the pot.

4. Water the plant and soil.

5. If using vermiculite, sprinkle on top of the soil to help retain the moisture.

Follow the instructions on the seed or plant label. Always have a demonstration example for the student to look at. This is a good activity for learning sequences. If at first a plant gets planted upside down in the soil, take a step back and ask the student whether they think the plant will grow upside down. Help them to look at your demonstration plant and replant the correct way. Be positive about what they do. Don't forget to water the plant at the end and if you have purchased some vermiculite, add some to the top of the soil around the cuttings or seeds. This gives optimal growing conditions for your seeds or cuttings. You do not need to use vermiculite in all garden beds and borders, just for starting off seeds and cuttings in small pots. I always sow or plant some extras as there will be plants that get squashed or dropped and ones that the cat ate at home!

Finally, let them take one plant home as a real motivator and reward.

Activity 5: Cooking activities in the spring

Aim
To form a connection with the garden and learn which herbs and plants to harvest for culinary use.

Growing radishes and beans
If you plant early enough you will be able to eat radishes and beans in late spring! In British Columbia we can sow radishes direct into the soil at the beginning of March and under cover in February. Broad beans can be sown in February if the soil is workable. See the vegetable growing chart on the West Coast Seeds website (www.westcoastseeds.com/productdetail/Gardening-Books/posters/poster-set) for further details about when to plant in British Columbia. In the UK, Garden Organic's website (www.gardenorganic.org.uk/growyourown/easiest.php) has easy to use and free to download charts, which will tell you when to direct sow seeds. You may be surprised to see what you can sow directly into the ground as early as March! Alternatively, check with your local gardening group to find out when they start planting outside. They will be able to tell you the usual timeframes for planting most of your vegetable crop.

Making a potato salad
Boil and halve some small white potatoes. Leave them aside to cool.

Harvest radishes and beans, and consider adding some lettuce and onion.

Slice up the radishes and beans. Add them to the potatoes and add butter, a squeeze of lemon juice and a splash of olive oil. Serve with a large piece of crusty bread. Enjoy your snack after digging in the garden!

Making herb butter

Collect a selection of evergreen herbs such as thyme, rosemary and sage. Crush or rip up the leaves with fingers and/or a pestle and mortar in separate bowls. Mix two teaspoons of one herb into 125g of unsalted softened butter. Beat with a fork until well mixed. With the back of a spoon, press the butter mixed with the herbs into some wax paper. Press the butter into either a roll or a small block and label. Place in the fridge for a few days to allow the herbs to settle in the butter and then remove to taste with a cracker. Have some water nearby to refresh oneself, and encourage tasting of all the different types of herb butter. Discuss the nutritional benefits of herbs such as the vitamins and minerals they contain.

Activity 6: Cooking activities in the summer

Aim

Enhancing food nutrition programmes in an outdoor setting.

Making pesto

Purchase basil leaves or harvest them from your garden. Mix two cups of fresh basil leaves with half a cup of olive oil and two minced garlic cloves. If you like, add pine nuts and a squeeze of lemon. Mix in a blender or with a hand grinder, and serve with salad or pasta. Basil has many benefits, including being a very good source of iron, calcium, potassium and vitamins C and K. It is also a good source of dietary fibre. (Caution: the smell of crushed garlic can be overwhelming to some ASD students.) If you don't have basil, chervil is a good herb replacement and is easy to grow.

Making pizza

Grow a pizza garden using a container planted with cherry tomatoes, basil and chives. Spread a ready-made pizza base with tomato paste, top with grated cheese, and cook as per the instructions on the pizza base packing. If you are working with a child who dislikes tomato paste, try drizzling olive oil on the pizza base before sprinkling with cheese. Add the basil, cherry tomatoes and chives after the base is cooked. Then take a break in the garden enjoying your fresh pizza!

Harvesting berries

Take a bag or container and go outside looking for blackberries. Be careful as they are very thorny. Why not plant a native berry border in your school garden to help teach identification and to have a nearby source of berries? You can purchase thornless blackberries to grow in the garden. Consider other naturalized edible berries too, such as huckleberries, cranberries, raspberries and blueberries (depending on which are native to you!). Look at the tiny seeds within the flesh of the berry, and discuss how seeds travel and the nutritional benefits of berries in our diets. Make a blackberry crumble, jam or jelly. There is so much you can do with berries!

Activity 7: Cooking activities in the autumn

Aim

To gain an understanding of the concept of seasonal harvesting.

Harvesting pumpkin seeds in October

Pumpkins are ready to harvest when the skin is hard and they sound hollow when you tap them. Using a sharp knife, cut the pumpkin in half and then into quarters. Scoop out the fleshy fibrous parts and all the seeds with a spoon, putting the seeds in a sieve. Examine the seeds with the children and drain them under the tap. Wash the pulp away from the seeds and dry them for one week on a paper towel. Once the seeds have dried, save some of them in an airtight container for planting next year, and roast the seeds you have left. Pumpkin seeds are a good source of iron and zinc, and of omega-3 fatty acids. With the remaining flesh of the pumpkin make a pumpkin pie, muffins or soup.

Planting bulbs

Autumn is the perfect time to plant garlic bulbs. Follow the planting instructions as per the packet. Advise the child not to eat the bulbs. When harvesting the following June/July, note that garlic has a powerful smell and can be overwhelming for ASD learners.

Saving tomato seeds

Be prepared to get a little messy as this method uses the process of fermentation. Harvest your tomatoes when they are ripe (red). If they are not ripe yet, bring them inside and place them on a tray on top of your washer/dryer and they will ripen quickly.

Cut a tomato in half from stem to blossom end. Observe the seeds in the middle. Using a spoon or fingers, scoop out the seeds and place in a cup or container. You could also just squeeze the seeds into a cup which is quite satisfying. Add a few tablespoons of water to the cup. Cover with plastic wrap and prick a small hole in the plastic wrap to allow air in to aid fermentation. You can also use a paper towel. Leave the cup for three days, stirring the mixture once daily. After three days the top of the surface will look mouldy but the seeds will have sunk to the bottom. Prepare your students for a bad smell when you remove the container cover. This process frees the seeds from any potential diseases. Remove the top scum and then rinse the seeds several times with a sieve under cold water. Place the seeds on a coffee filter or wax paper to dry. Once dried (not sticky), store them in a glass container in a fridge if possible. Sow the seeds the following spring.

Activity 8: Cooking activities in the winter

Aim

To continue to entice students into the garden all through the year.

Vegetable soup

Use some or all of the vegetables below to make a fat free soup. Feel free to substitute with whatever vegetables you have growing. This sign * indicates what you must have. Each vegetable measurement should be 225g.

peeled carrots, cut into 5cm length

leeks, halved and cut into 5cm length

peeled swede, cut into 5cm length

1 small onion, chopped*

1.5 litres of hot vegetable stock*

3 bay leaves

Preheat oven to 300° Farenheit or 150° Celsius (Gas Mark 2). Place all the ingredients into a casserole dish. Cover, and allow to simmer gently in the lowest part of the oven for up to three hours. If you have added bay leaves remove them, and then puree the soup. Gently re-heat and serve in soup bowls. If you like, sprinkle some chopped herbs such as chives or parsley on top.

In the summer, you could substitute the vegetables for fresh herbs such as chives, mint, sage, rosemary and sorrel. Cube some potatoes and cook in 25g of butter, then add to the vegetable stock and herbs.

Tasting citrus fruits

Buy or, if you are lucky enough to live somewhere hot enough, harvest some oranges and lemons. Slice them in half with the student watching. Encourage the student to first try squeezing the citrus fruits and then to taste the juice. I tell stories about how pirates used to suck on oranges to keep away scurvy. You might want to print off some pictures of pirates as a visual cue. Learning the value of eating citrus fruits, which are high in vitamin C, also helps nutritional awareness.

Edible Valentine arrangements

Get a mug or cup with a handle for ease of carrying (from a thrift store or an old one of your own). Place a small floral brick (a foam block used for flower arranging and available from craft stores or florists) inside and purchase or bring in edible plants and herbs, such as parsley or coriander. Consider adding strawberries on sticks, lingonberries (sour but edible) and a little Valentine message that you can cut out or draw and clip onto the side of the mug. Encourage the students to taste the plants as they create their arrangement and then to give the mug to their teacher, a parent or friend in an act of loving kindness. Ask the child to note the reaction of the person they give it to. It may be a good idea to give the teacher forewarning that this will happen so they are prepared to stop instructing for a moment to give due thanks. In this moment of appreciation real self-esteem is being built.

Activity 9: Going on field trips

Aim

Providing opportunities for educational development and exposure to a wide diversity of plants at different locations. You could use these field trips to purchase plants for cooking activities. Field trips can be used as a reward for good behaviour.

The activity

Visits to the local garden centre are highly motivating and exciting. Allow sufficient time to walk around outside the nursery looking at trees, shrubs and aquatic features. Water features are a source of fascination for children. The ASD learner may find going inside a garden nursery or centre too invigorating on their first visit, particularly around plants which are very fragrant, such as hyacinths or lilies. When exploring plant scents be careful of sensory overload. If the student becomes too disturbed, take them to the exit and resume your walk outside. This way you're reaffirming a positive association with the garden centre and the student will have time to recover and relax.

Ask if a member of staff will be available to show you around, which will give you the added safety of having someone to steer your students away from any poisonous plants in the nursery. Regular trips will get easier and easier. Go in small groups often.

You don't have to go far to enjoy a field trip. All around you is your natural flora and fauna and you won't need to sort out permission slips if you stay on school grounds. Take a seasonal walk around the school. Can you identify the trees in your streets? In spring are the cherry trees blooming? Can you spot the bright yellow flowers on the forsythia shrub? In summer, what fruits and flowers are all around us? In autumn, observe which trees have dropped their leaves. As you walk gather sticks, seeds and cones, feel them and note how they look. Consider taking pictures of trees and plants around your school, laminating the sheet and then asking the children to match the pictures to the plants. This is a nature treasure hunt and fun to do with a buddy.

I arrive in spring!   *I like the shade*

Count my petals   *Woof woof is close to my name*

I like to climb structures   *I am huge!*

Nature treasure hunt in the spring

Conclusion

A horticultural programme complements the inclusive environment that support teams provide in schools. This nature based approach is also recommended in many resource books and articles in relation to other special educational needs. By introducing, maintaining and nurturing a garden, positive building supports are created. Digging, finding bugs, watching the birds, creating a home for many animals and being part of a group – a garden club is a very satisfying reward. This is fundamentally nurture by nature in practice. Please do consider incorporating gardening into your child's individual education plan.

Chapter 5

Anxiety, Anger and Depression

Our fears strangle us, stop us in our paths and inhibit our capacity for self-awareness. Imagine you're standing in the middle of a forest fire immobilized with fear, not knowing which way to turn. We are so distracted by our fears that we can no longer listen to what our body and mind are telling us. Mindfulness teaches us to try to catch our anger in its early stages, as if we're holding a match in our hands about to light the fire in our minds. Through horticultural therapy activities we can experience the flow of senses (necessary to awaken a sense of aliveness) and learn how to deal with our fears through the dual track of mind and body attention.

Approach

DISTRACTION

Gardening activities such as weeding (a well-reported therapeutic activity) are mentally absorbing tasks. Add to this the movement involved in weeding (reaching, bending, pulling, digging) and you've got your brain and body fully in sync and focused on the task in hand. While working away weeding we're subconsciously analysing experiences, fears and anxieties without realizing it. You're so engrossed in your task that you're also probably very happy. At the end of the activity we have instilled a sense of anticipation and hope. Will our seedlings grow? Will we remember to check on them regularly? Will the work we did today pay off as we watch tiny seedlings grow into beautiful plants? This is nurture through nature and distraction from our anxieties.

EXERCISE

Exercise is the go-to therapy in many countries for anxiety and depression. For me the garden is everything. It is not only a sensory gym, but also a cerebral and physical gym. Lifting, carrying, digging, planting and raking are all physically demanding activities. What makes the difference is that while I'm doing all these activities, I'm also learning. Educating oneself about soil, plant names, when to prune, when not to prune, learning how to identify good bugs from bad bugs, how to plant, when to plant: the list goes on and on. My brain neurons are firing away!

Through exercise we're reducing muscle tension which leads to reduced feelings of anxiety. Exercise also increases serotonin. Serotonin regulates signals to the brain, improving the performance of the prefrontal cortex to inhibit fear and install a sense of calm. Through a positive association with a physical activity, we're retraining the brain's plasticity over time. A racing heartbeat and raised breathing are no longer associated with an anxiety attack but with the positive association of digging a trench for potatoes or pulling up an old shrub with stubborn roots.

The *Vancouver Sun* (2010) reported that as we work in soil, bacteria are released that increase our serotonin levels. This is another good reason to add gardening to a special needs programme within schools.

I hope this book will teach you that when you're feeling anxious, you need to get outside into the garden. What a beautiful society we would live in if everyone tended to their gardens in moments of sadness or anxiety rather than taking drugs or alcohol.

We're also preparing our children for a better lifestyle as they grow old. The importance of exercise in staving off dementia and other illnesses is well researched. If we can stay active by gardening as long as possible, we will slow down the degeneration of the brain.

SELF-AWARENESS

While gardening we're learning not only factual information but also more about ourselves. We're learning that we love the taste of fresh parsley, but hate the smell of lavender, even if everyone else seems to like it. We hate weeding but we love watering. I find that young people discover similarities with family members never before realized until working in the garden. These memories are stimulated in context. For example I have heard: 'Grandma likes to garden too… Now I think about it my uncle likes to mow the lawn…' We're discovering that we have something in common, a talking point. Encourage children to invite their family and friends into the garden to show them around.

In seniors' homes the garden may be the final place that seniors and their families have in common: as short-term memories degenerate, a long-term memory of a particular variety of rose or the fragrance of the lilac remain. These long-term memories are stimulated in a garden. It's an emotionally safe neutral meeting place where experiences can be shared.

This self-awareness comes with being given the time not only to talk but also to do something we love to do in a calm, peaceful and yet interesting environment. While working in the garden, ask the children to observe emotions and, if possible, write them down. Through this new self-awareness we gain greater insight and we can begin to look deeper along the path to becoming a more caring individual towards family and friends.

A note on medication

Taking medication can be a bone of contention and a source of embarrassment. It may be helpful for your child to know that gardeners amend their soil all the time. Soil pH measures the acidity or alkalinity of a soil. At a pH of 7 (neutral), acidity and alkalinity are balanced. If our soil is too acidic we can add lime to balance the pH; in order to add nourishment to our plants we may have to add fertilizer to amend the pH level. Similarly, we may have to take medication for a period to nourish our bodies. The goal of adding fertilizer to our plants is to try to meet the needs of the plant. We don't always get this right, and taking medication can be the same. Sometimes, we have to try a few different methods and regulate the amount before we find success.

Plants as continual adolescents

Plants are much like adolescents in that plants emit chemicals (hormones) and continually sprout new growth, ever changing with the seasons. Both plants and humans have different needs in different seasons. Plants have learned to let go of their fruits and dead branches – we can learn from them. Many people feel a release of negative influences as they watch the leaves fall from a tree. Plants have their unique forms, colours and personalities just like adolescents.

Sexual reproduction

Plants are continually sexually active. Making fruit and/or seeds is really all they do. Plants reproduce the same way as humans do. A female plant requires the pollen from a male plant to fertilize her eggs in her ovary in order to produce seeds. It may be less embarrassing for some children and easier for you to touch on the subject of reproduction through the plant analogy first, and then examine the similarities to the human reproduction system. A large poppy is a good plant to dissect and examine the male and female parts of a flower.

Imagine seeds like little children being ejected into the world with their embryo (baby plant) surrounded by a coat of nutritious energy (packed lunch) and a hard protective coat to protect them until the right conditions (weather and temperature) for germination. If you think about it, the seed stage is the only time in a plant's life it will travel. Seeds are a fascinating topic which might capture the curiosity of some adolescents. Some seeds can be dormant for over 200 years, then if the soil is stirred up and in the right conditions, they will successfully germinate into healthy plants. There are plants that survive through the use of water, such as ferns and mosses. There is a wealth of books on the subject of plant strategies to spread their seeds and ensure germination. For further reading, I particularly recommend *Seeds, Time Capsules of Life* by Rob Kesseler and Wolfgang Stuppy (2006).

A note on communication

We all want our children to be happy and feel safe and secure free from anxiety and sadness. However, the stresses of modern life are taking a toll on our children. It is important to note that anger, anxiety and depression are all painful states of mind and in a school environment gardening is a perfect outlet for a student's physical and emotional needs. As a horticultural therapist I concentrate on physical activities rather than meditation with youth. Imagine asking a child with a child with behavioural issues to meditate when they've just spent an hour sitting at a desk doing maths. Not only is this frustrating for the child, eyeing the digging plot keenly, but also for many children it is just too dull. Meditation may also reveal some unsettling emotions which will be very difficult to process on their own. If children ask to meditate, by all means find them a quiet place under a tree or beside a water feature for them to do this.

Children under the age of eight find it very difficult to express themselves in words so it is good practice to develop ways to communicate nonverbally. Encourage the use of hand signals such as the thumbs up and thumbs down signs. Have a picture with a variety of facial expressions they can point at to give you an indication of their mood. This is helpful for assessing the level of difficulty they may be experiencing. I also encourage students to write on stones and pebbles, placing them in a fountain, perhaps making a wish as they do this.

If you haven't yet read Chapter 3 on 'Why Dig?', please do so. Digging is the first and foremost introduction to exercise in the garden and to me the most meaningful way to introduce young people to the joys of gardening.

Anxiety

Plants grow at their own pace, not at the pace we demand of them. I think they're very cool like that. As a gardener I have learned to take nothing for granted. We should take a lesson from them and allow our children to find their own pace as a unique flower.

Once supervising a lady bug craft painting table for preschoolers, I was amazed at how many parents (who were impatient to move on to the next table) took over the painting from their preschoolers and finished the craft themselves. Before this moment, I had never realized how controlling as parents we can be. I made a concerted effort to observe future craft sessions and it was the same again and again. In this example, you can see how we're denying our child's creativity right from preschool.

A garden can provide:

- a calm, restful and undisturbed environment that any anxious child deserves
- the opposite of anxiety, which is serenity
- sounds of water and nature, such as bird song and bees buzzing around
- no disturbing people
- a wild area such as a digging plot with weeds and fungi, tree roots and worms
- a special place to rest and contemplate our emotions
- somewhere to feel a sense of outside
- a place to hide and seek refuge in a shed, by the compost heap or in a tree fort
- a sense of self-worth and control
- an opportunity of being part of a group (garden club), which helps reduce feelings of hopelessness commonly experienced by youth
- opportunities for social interaction if wanted
- solitary activities such as working on pruning, pricking out and planting seedlings
- opportunities for creativity and self-expression (garden design and botanical art).

AIMS OF GARDENING ACTIVITY FOR CHILDREN WITH ANXIETY

Children with anxiety will benefit from gardening activities in the following ways:

- having time to check out the garden, to see what has changed
- having time alone on a regular basis or as demanded
- training their attention to focus on the task in hand
- providing an outlet for creativity and self-expression
- being kind to themselves when their mind or attention wanders and gently being steered back to the activity with compassion and understanding
- understanding that emotions rise and will eventually pass away
- observing their emotions, naming them and making a note of them
- recognizing that it is futile to worry about the future as sometimes we cannot change it any more than we can the past
- finding a sense of joy and motivation in the garden through our connection with Mother Earth.

Anger

Gardening is a good outlet for physical aggression. If we cling to our anger we will only find a path of suffering. Students need to learn how to let go of their anger and whatever particular fixation they may have in order to move forward with a healthy mind. Plants can show us many examples of letting go. Fruit trees drop their fruit, deciduous trees let their leaves fall every autumn. Trees drop their seeds and cones and annual plants grow, flower and die all in one year. As we watch trees drop their leaves each autumn, we should take this cue to let go of our angers and anxieties. The ceaseless unfolding of nature's cycles shows us pertinently that life has its ups and downs and we cannot affect this in any way. This is the fundamental notion of interrelatedness in not only the mindfulness approach but also many other cultures.

A helpful visualization is to imagine our mind as a big blue sky. The clouds (emotions, thoughts and sensations observed and explored) that are gathering in our mind sky should be encouraged to pass on by. In this way we are letting go of fixations leading to anger.

AIMS OF GARDENING ACTIVITY FOR CHILDREN WITH ANGER

Children with anger will benefit from gardening activities in the following ways:

- doing rigorous gardening tasks such as raking, digging, carrying pots, and weeding stubborn plants to alleviate physical aggression tendencies and lessen muscle tension

- being aware of their own mind and body (how did I feel before coming out into the garden and then how did I feel afterwards?)

- becoming aware of a reoccurring theme that is a trigger to anger

- visualizing an activity in the garden can be helpful to tame anger rising in classroom environment

- experiencing and mastering a pleasurable activity

- providing a sense of independence

- having opportunities for problem solving

- accepting responsibility for a plant

- learning to give and to receive feedback.

Depression

Exercise is the go-to therapy for depression. Gardening activities can be gentle initially, such as arranging a fragrant bouquet of flowers. This is a good activity to start with and will lead up to more rigorous activities as a way to overcome feelings of lethargy. Over time our minds and bodies strengthen sufficiently to generate energy for taking action in our lives. By detaching ourselves from the illness of depression, we can learn positive associations with exercise and gardening.

AIMS OF GARDENING ACTIVITY FOR CHILDREN WITH DEPRESSION

Children with depression will benefit from gardening activities in the following ways:

- offering them a place of refuge and being able to stay clear of areas with high social interaction until their mental health is restored

- giving them the time to work on an activity without feeling rushed

- enjoying some peace and quiet and listening to the birds sing

- providing areas for contemplation, maybe on a seat by a fountain or water feature

- providing reasons to be positive

- becoming aware of the seasons and the cycle of life in the garden

- observing a compost heap: compost heaps are areas of great fascination, and separating the red wriggler worms from the compost is a very engrossing activity

- benefiting from teachers remaining flexible and adaptable to their interests

- being educated on the benefits of good nutrition and how we can improve our mood by using our bodies to cure our brains.

- utilizing the natural environment around them for sensory stimulation; for example, standing in a ray of sunlight can instantly warm our hearts and minds

- discovering that plants need light energy to produce chemicals, a by-product of which is oxygen (just as we humans need fresh air, sunshine and exercise to get our brains working and taking in oxygen)

- understanding the process of photosynthesis (which I think helps children become aware that we need to understand human biology, how our bodies work and what we need for good health and nutrition).

Tips for engaging students

If a child seems really uninterested in joining in, try to find something that you think might engage them.

THE VENUS FLY TRAP

Did you know that plants can count? The venus fly trap will wait until the second movement from a fly on her leaf before she closes together to slowly digest the fly's nutrients. After 12 hours, if the prey has escaped or is too small, the trap will reopen.

Suggest having a go at growing a venus fly trap (sow the seeds inside as they are tiny and may be blown away outside) or purchasing one for the school. What other carnivorous plants are there? Consider having a carnivorous plant themed container garden. See Appendix 5 on themed containers and gardens.

BLOWING BUBBLES

Buy a bubble blower! By blowing bubbles around your garden or nature setting you can demonstrate the concept of thigmomorphogenesis (the response by plants to wind, raindrops and the passing of invertebrates and other animals to alter their growth patterns). This fun activity teaches us to observe not only which way the wind is blowing that day but also how the bubbles touch plants. By touching the plants we simulate the wind and learn how raindrops or passing animals that touch plants are helping plants to alter their growth patterns. Through this concept (discovered in the 1970s by M.J. Jaffe; see Jaffe 1973), botanists discovered that plants grown in a greenhouse tend to be taller and more spindly than plants that grow outside in our garden. The regular rubbing or bending of plant stems by the wind and rain inhibits their growth upwards but makes shorter, stockier plants better adapted to survive in their environment.

Observe the bubbles floating up and away. Watch how this is a source of fascination for children of all ages and special needs.

- Point out how high the bubbles rise.

- Is it windy or not?

- Is the sun in your eyes while you watch the bubbles rise?

- Which direction is the wind blowing? Introduce the compass: North, South, East and West.

- Watch how the bubbles land on plants and touch them. This sense of touch is helping to strengthen the plants.

Discussion points in the garden

Here is a list of points for discussion with young people:

- winter and early spring: cooking, Christmas wreaths, dried flower arrangements and herbs

- spring and summer: flowers; structure; pollination and fertilization; native plants

- summer and autumn: fruits and seeds; cycle of plant growth; cycle of seasons; collecting and storing seeds

- autumn: planting bulbs, pruning trees, perusing seed catalogues and ordering seeds

- plant names (how many plants have animal names?)

- what animals are in the garden

- garden design and contemporary art

- what's in the compost heap: bug hunt

- how scientists look at nature for solutions to everyday problems: check out the Ask Nature website (www.asknature.org).

Activities

Use compassion with students with anxiety, as often they present themselves as disinterested or non-communicative. Do not control everything that happens in the garden: the students may want to dig first and then see what you have planned for them. Allowing them some autonomy will help you gain their trust. If the sun is shining why not take a moment to enjoy the sun's warmth, like a busy bee getting ready to fly? Try to remain flexible like a tree in the wind.

Activity 1: Create a flower

Aim

Providing an outlet for creativity and self-expression while also learning about basic botany.

Tools

You will need the following items:

- examples of a range of flowers and plants and, if possible, some previously drawn pictures from other children
- paper
- pens.

The activity

Explain to the children that there are many different plants in our environment. Some plants thrive in the shade, some in the sun. Some are evergreen, some deciduous (shed their leaves each year). Ask the children to consider and draw what type of flower they would be and if they are able, label the plant parts: roots, stem which supports the flower, petals and male and female parts.

Always have a demonstration plant available or examples of other children's drawings for reference. If this is too difficult for some, encourage the children to find an example in the garden to show you.

If you have time, sit around in a circle afterwards and ask the children to share their drawings with each other. They may find similarities in what they have drawn. By doing such an activity we learn more about ourselves, our likes and our dislikes.

Leonardo da Vinci wrote about mixing sounds, smells and sight in his ideal garden. Leonardo was much inspired by nature. Through art we can help students express their emotions that they may otherwise be unable to put into words. Adolescent expression is emotional and the energy can be positive or negative. Creating our own flower is an easy way to express our individuality and art is a perfect avenue as a symbolic mode of self-expression.

You may find that some of the drawings are disturbing. It is important to remain non-judgemental and to encourage self-expression through art. Reassure the child that it is good to be truthful, because recognizing our fears and anxieties is the path to the healing process.

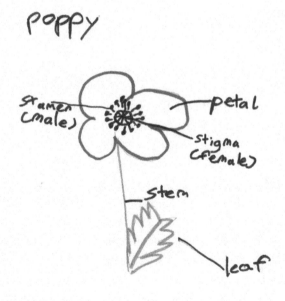

Plant parts drawn by eight-year-old girl

Activity 2: Bug art activity

Aim

Learning that in life there is joy and sorrow, and exploring positive and negative feelings and emotions.

Tools

You will need the following items:

- paper and pens

- pictures of beneficial insects: lady bugs, butterflies, bees and ground beetles

- pictures of garden pests: slugs, snails (although children see snails in a positive light on the whole), mosquitoes.

The activity

Take a walk around the garden and see if you can spot any insects or other garden invertebrates. Find a quiet place to sit down (ideally a grassy area). Sitting quietly in a nature setting is very inspirational. Ask the children to consider if they have any fears. A fear is a worry or something that makes us nervous. Explain that it is helpful to draw a picture of our fears so we can better visualize and identify them, and subsequently deal with them. This activity helps to connect emotions with feelings. Emotions are strong feelings such as joy or anger. Feelings can be the capacity to experience a sense of touch, for example.

There may be some resistance to acknowledging any fears, in which case stick to the horticultural theme of understanding and distinguishing beneficial insects from pests in the garden.

I give the example of my most common concern, slugs. I worry that slugs will eat all my lettuces in the vegetable plot. Even if children have never gardened before, they usually seem to understand this concern and so this makes perfect sense. However, I have a helper bug that is a butterfly. When my helper bug sees my worry bug, she flies down and squashes my worry bug slug flat! I often have to repeat this part a few times, as hearing about a helper bug is a new concept to children.

If this activity is successful, encourage the students to keep a journal of their experiences throughout the seasons. Both teacher and student should make a note of which garden activities they find unpleasant and which they find pleasant. Try to ensure you direct their attention back to the senses that are stimulated. How does drawing your worry bug make you feel? Did you know you have a helper bug? Are you having difficulty visualizing your helper bug?

Base information on facts: for example, all insects have six legs. Spiders are not insects: they have eight legs! When information is shared in context, it is easier to learn. You may want to do another activity which involves sticking the correct number of legs on pictures of beneficial insects and spiders on pop sticks and decorating the garden or containers with them.

You may get drawings of all kinds of monsters. That is just fine. Reward the children for their drawings and mastery of their emotions. This activity should promote a positive growth experience. Understanding feelings is a valuable exercise in awareness of our own emotions and behaviour and how we can change them. By looking at the drawings in a group, children gain a better understanding and empathy for others which can lead to deepening friendships.

Activity 3: Lavender bags

Aim
Deliberately shifting focus away from thinking and into the senses to calm the mind.

Tools
You will need the following items:

- silk or cotton craft bags

- dried lavender (harvest flower stems from lavender twice a year and allow them to air dry in a garage).

The activity
This is a perfect wintertime activity. Sit a group of children around a large pile of dried lavender and give them a demonstration. Break off the flowers and discard the stems. Later add the stems to the compost. Add a handful of lavender flowers to each bag. Consider adding a tag with the name of your garden club on it and selling them at a school event or giving them to friends and family as gifts.

Lavender is a calming fragrance. By working with the herb with our hands, we're initiating the sensory flow. As the students immerse themselves in this activity, explain some facts to the group:

- Lavender is a small aromatic evergreen shrub with narrow strong smelling leaves and bluish purple flowers.

- Lavender is a medicinal herb used for centuries and has many therapeutic uses for anxiety, insomnia, burns, migraine headaches and indigestion.

- The most fragrant lavender is English lavender, but there are other varieties such as French and Spanish.

- Cook with lavender: consider making lavender shortbread (see recipe on p.94).

- Lavender has a high nectar content and is much loved by bees.

- Lavender loves sunshine.

You may need to open a window after a while as the fragrance from the flowers can become quite overwhelming.

Activity 4: The multisensory guessing game

Aim
Taking part in a multisensory game with cognitive, emotional and spiritual benefits.

Tools
You will need the following items:

- paper bags or ziplock bags for holding the seeds

- two types of peas or beans (use large ones, for example green peas, broad beans, soya beans or mung beans)

- or use large seeds such as sunflower, corn seeds or seed cones.

The activity
This game is useful for group counseling sessions. Divide the group into pairs. Give one person the bag with the seeds in and ask them to close their eyes. Then ask them to take one seed out at a time and guess which one it is. If they are having difficulty, they can pass the seed to their partner, who will help them guess. They then pass the bag to their partner to take their turn. This game is multisensory and helps children learn to cooperate together. I find this activity to be a lot of fun too. The children are often surprised to see how much they get right without looking, which is a source of great accomplishment. We're exploring and learning to use our other senses.

If you have used sprouting beans such as mung beans, encourage the children to lay them on a damp paper towel (soak the beans for as long as you can beforehand) and they should sprout within a couple of days. Encourage the children to taste the sprouts and discuss their nutritional value. Sprouting seeds provide the most immediate form of gratification you will encounter in the plant sprouting world.

Activity 5: Planting seeds

Aim
Learning the basics of seed sowing and exploring actions and consequences.

Tools
You will need the following items:

- seeds such as radish or bean seeds
- flower pots, yoghurt pots (with drainage holes) or egg cartons
- larger containers
- potting soil
- vermiculite (if available)
- watering can.

The activity
Run a demonstration of the sequence of sowing seeds:

1. Fill three-quarters of the pot with potting soil.
2. Sprinkle seeds thinly.
3. Cover with more potting soil and/or vermiculite.
4. Water seeds.

Follow the instructions on your seed packets. In February you can sow most seeds inside. In the spring many seeds can be sown directly in the garden. If working in a group there is no need to individually label the pots, or the plot if you are direct sowing seeds, with the names of the children. It is better to have a communal pot or flower bed, so any individual fears of a seed not germinating are removed. Children are very competitive naturally and will compare their plants. It is inevitable someone will point out the plant that did not make it, which can be a little bit hard on whoever planted it.

Radishes will sprout within a week inside and, dependent on the spring weather you are encountering, within two to three weeks outside. As the seedlings emerge they resemble little hearts.

We all want our plants to grow big and strong. We're naturally competitive and that is a survival trait. Sometimes, when sowing seeds we realize that even though we did all we could to provide optimal growing conditions, through either the weather or a foot that has strayed off the path our plants did not grow as well as we had expected. We learn that the consequences to our actions are not always predictable. Accepting change is very hard. We watered the plant every day so why did it die? We ask ourselves what we could do differently next time. We're looking for a solution, which is a positive state of mind.

Consider running a relaxation exercise or meditation prior to planting (see Appendix 6).

Activity 6: Flower arranging

Aim

Realizing we have choices, being creative as a source of accomplishment, stimulating an interest in garden materials and interacting with plants and people.

Tools

You will need the following items:

- mugs to carry arrangement home in
- floral foam bricks
- a variety of flowers (avoid roses which have prickly stems).

The activity

We feel good when we work with plants and everyone likes to receive flowers; however, very few children are given the opportunity to work with flowers. Try your local supermarkets or flower shops for out-of-date blooms they may be willing to give you for free. Maybe you're working on a theme such as green for St Patrick's Day or red for Valentine's Day. Have a demonstration arrangement completed and also demonstrate placing the floral foam brick in the mug and provide some suggestions on how to arrange flowers.

If a child is tense when starting this activity, ask them to notice which parts of their body feel tense and to imagine their breath going into and out of the area of tightness. Once the activity is ended, ask them whether their body feels calmer and less tight.

An act of kindness would be to then give this arrangement to a friend or teacher. Ask the student to observe the reaction of the recipient and later ask the student how this made them feel. Did they get satisfaction from the delight of the recipient, for example?

Chapter 6

Attention Deficit Hyperactivity Disorder

Approach

Taking a child with ADHD outside into a garden that you are not familiar with may be considered risky. Therefore I have included an example of a risk assessment in Appendix 2. See also Chapter 9 on poisonous plants. I would encourage you to find a teacher or parent volunteer with gardening experience to help you identify and remove all the toxic plants from the garden.

A garden can create a connected environment for a child with ADHD. There is an emotional connection to the place and to the people in it. Feelings can be explored in a neutral and safe environment while children play, explore, and gain mastery and achievement in the activities they do in the garden. View your garden as a 'science laboratory' that will provide additional opportunities for a child with ADHD to be industrious and learn a competency. Learning about science and maths in context is good common sense. Also, I believe learning in a different environment helps with improved memory recall and associations. Through these additional experiences children encounter situations where they learn to consider alternative courses of action and control impulses. Controlling those impulses is an essential skill to maintain friendships and those friendships are essential to the joy of childhood.

In life some days are better than others. Assessing whether a child is going to cooperate with another child in the garden can sometimes be difficult. My approach for the most part is that even though there may be conflicts and tension I'd rather work through these social moments than be working with a solitary child in the garden. Children mindfully often call out and name their emotions and feelings. It's hard to keep up some days. 'He took my shovel – now I'm bored… She's upsetting me… He's not the boss of me…' And so on…

Try to acknowledge each emotion as the children experience them and recognize another child's attempt to problem solve an issue or offer negotiation. Sometimes, you might not want to get involved at all and just take a step back and see which child tries to placate the tension. You can reward them for their efforts later on. However, there are days when a child with ADHD, who perhaps did not get much sleep, may well benefit from regular quiet time (albeit supervised) in the garden. Freedom to choose and to roam in the garden is essential for peace of mind. It is also time for the support teacher or parent/carer to take a moment to relax and to take a mental break.

If a child is particularly agitated I would recommend going for a rigorous walk around the school (maybe twice!) before gardening.

The carer for a child with ADHD I have worked with for two years told me the child had started to ask to walk to school in the morning. I was so pleased as this means this child has learned enough self-awareness to recognize and to advocate some exercise in their schedule. At the end of the conversation the carer laughed and admitted she felt better for walking too. It's never too late to learn the positive benefits of exercise.

Benefits of gardening for a child with ADHD

There are several benefits of gardening for children with ADHD, including the following:

- *Psychological:* spending time in nature increases focus and attention; creating a curious mind; perseverance.

- *Cognitive:* controlled thinking leading to less distractibility and impulsivity; problem solving with peers; classification; reading instructions; putting things together.

- *Educational:* science (life cycles of plants, plant identification and pest control) and maths (planting instructions, seed germination, climate control and water or fertilizer measurement).

- *Emotional:* sharing positive experiences with adults and peers; providing opportunities for peer interaction and relationships; improved self-esteem; excess energy channelled into constructive activities; opportunities to cooperate on tasks; improved empathy through nurturing plants; greater sense of responsibility for actions; acceptance for situations; controlling impulses, which is very important as children who are hyperactive experience difficulty sustaining healthy peer interactions.

- *Prevocational work skills:* focusing on directions, learning a sequence and staying on task; acquiring horticultural skills; plant identification; processing feedback; sharing accomplishments.

Building parental rapport

By working alongside your child in the garden you can work on improving your understanding of your child and also learn how discouraging daily experiences for a child with ADHD can be. By showing an interest and playing with your child in the garden, you are helping to work on countering negative experiences with positive messages, which will really help your child's self-esteem. I believe building self-esteem is key to providing the right state of mind for a child to develop and learn successfully. Try to be positive at all times. Even if your child plants a plant upside down maybe have some fun with this rather than instantly remarking 'You did that wrong' or a similar negative comment. You may be surprised to note how many times a child hears 'No' in one day.

Allowing your child to decide the gardening activity they do that day is important. It might be a little frustrating to you if you had planned to get them to weed the garden for you and they decide to plant or dig instead but freedom of choice is an important self-esteem building tool.

The garden is the perfect environment to teach self-control. For example, having a variety of seeds from which to choose to plant means a child must use reading, problem-solving and decision-making skills.

You can expand on working with any disciplinary issues you've been facing in the garden. Praise good behaviour as much as you can and try to let go of bad behaviour unless it is dangerous, such as hitting or throwing tools. This approach is called 'shaping' behaviour and by breaking tasks down into achievable ends success is guaranteed.

While working together in the garden notice how your mind will wander and roam and how any disruptive behaviour your child may have been experiencing has decreased. I hope that when you're having a bad day, suggesting going out into the garden becomes your tool to help calm down and reset your child rather than having to threaten a punishment.

Activities

Try to consider carefully the mix of children you take out into the garden. For example, a child who shouts a lot might not be a good companion for a child with ASD, who would spend most of their time with their hands over their ears. Keep the groups small if possible. As the children get used to one another and the garden and gain greater mastery over areas you can gradually increase the size of the group.

Activity 1: Breaking the ice game

Aim

Taking part in an ice breaker for a group of children, reducing aggressive behaviour and encouraging peer cooperation.

Tools

You will need the following items:

- outside open space, preferably fenced or courtyard garden
- your voice.

The activity

This is a fun ice breaker game for new friends, which makes you think quickly and will tire out fidgety and restless children. I recommend this game to support staff who have confined spaces to work with children outside. Many of us live in places where it rains a lot and quite often the garden can be slippery with wet leaves. In this game the child runs on the spot. Wet leaves should be cleared from the ground before you begin this activity.

Tell the children that they are going to play the bean game. The bean game involves acting out the characteristics of certain beans. Ask the children what beans they know. Give them time to consider. There is a Mexican jumping bean, a dwarf bean, a runner bean, a broad bean and so on. As the caller you call out the different beans and the children should act out the characteristics. Of course, you will need to join in as this makes it far more enjoyable for the children. Suggested characteristics are as follows:

- Mexican jumping bean: jumping

- dwarf bean: crouching down
- running bean: running on the spot
- broad bean: standing tall and proud and marching on the spot.

Following this activity, why not plant some beans? There are many types of beans. Broad beans (*Vicia faba*) can be planted in the autumn. They have no cholesterol, are high in protein and have very low fat content. Bush and pole beans (*Phaseolus vulgaris*) are high in dietary fibre, vitamin C and calcium. Some pole beans grow up to eight feet high, and the Purple peacock variety has purple seed pods. Runner beans (*Phaseolus coccineus*) prefer cool roots in the summer and require pollination by bees (or hummingbirds) to set seed so are good addition to a school garden.

Activity 2: Designing a garden for pollinators

Aim

Becoming aware of the role of pollinators, and of the structures and life cycle of plants, and using imagination and art in nature as a mode of self-expression and self-awareness.

Tools

You will need the following items:

- gardening magazines and books for inspiration (butterflies, bees and wasps)
- large pieces of paper
- felt-tip pens, crayons with bright colours.

The activity

Attracting beneficial insects into a garden is essential for our survival, and all children should learn this skill. Teach them the following five basic principles, which will help them to do this:

- The garden needs flowers in bloom most of the year, from early spring through to autumn.
- Flowers need to be a variety of sizes.
- Flowers need to have a variety of shapes for pollinators with long and short tongues.
- Composite flowers are best (such as sunflowers and daisies) rather than doubles.
- Fragrant flowers attract pollinators.

Without the process of pollination, a plant will not produce seeds. The gardener will have nothing to collect and will not be able to harvest and store the seeds for next year's planting. This is an essential skill for our survival.

Spread the books and magazines out and encourage the children to create on a large piece of paper their own garden full of flowers to attract pollinating insects to. Ask them to label (or have some prepared labels to stick on) which flowers attract bees, butterflies or wasps. Keep an open mind. Some children may draw flowers which they have created in their imagination rather than copying specific varieties. Do the children have a fresh perspective on the role of bees and butterflies?

Display these pictures in your school library or kitchen area at a height other children can view them. You could also ask the children to present their drawings to their class.

Activity 3: Gamer's themed container garden

Aim
Taking part in an outdoor activity that requires endurance and has uncertainties.

Tools
You will need the following items:

- container

- potting soil

- a variety of bright and bold plants: sunflowers, lilies, daisies, mixed with oddballs such as cacti and venus fly trap

- child's favourite characters such as the toys handed out with burgers, cereal packets or in chocolate eggs.

The activity

> 'In Super Mario flower power is the best power
> you can have!'
>
> *Boy aged 5*

There are more examples of themed containers and gardens in Appendix 5, but you are really only limited by your imagination. Getting outside and capturing a child's curiosity is really easy in a garden setting. Many children, particularly boys, also find much inspiration from action movies and video games and I use this as a tool to engage with them. Two boys in one garden club made a short film about an action frog. The frog was a bendy green plastic figure from the dollar store that I'd bought and hung from a hanging basket. Each week this frog was moved around lovingly by these two boys. At the end of the year one boy made a ninja costume for the frog at home. This must have taken him quite some time and perseverance. The film was two minutes long and showed the frog having adventures, naming plants and drinking nectar in the garden. It was highly entertaining and very illuminating to comprehend the extent of their horticultural knowledge from working in the garden for a year. I also understood (and it took me a year to grasp this!) that in this particular courtyard garden, to these two boys, the whole garden is action frog themed.

I have found that discussing the flora and fauna on video games is a way to connect and relate to certain children who like to discuss the games they have played and the various levels they've reached. These video games can be inspirational for visual learners and create self-esteem where the classroom environment does not. Game developers have figured out that very young children intuitively understand nature and plants and the importance of mushrooms!

Gamer's themed garden by a five-year-old boy

Preparing to make the gamer's themed container garden could involve a field trip to your local garden centre to purchase the plants together. The experience of playing the video games will fade but the memory of experiencing planting some beautiful scented plants will remain forever.

Ensure that due praise is given to the child that completes this activity and that enough time is factored in to have a discussion around their favourite video games.

Activity 4: An awareness game

Aim
Instilling a sense of outside and calmness, and improving focus, energy, creativity and auditory input.

Tools
You will need the following items:

- a place to sit outside

- paper, crayons and felt-tip pens.

The activity
Once outside, explain to the child that you are both going to play the listening game.

Explain that in order to hear all the sounds of nature we have to sit and observe quietly. Now close your eyes and listen! Try to identify the noises you hear. Is it a blackbird or a blue jay singing? An aeroplane circling or a teacher shouting?

Ensure you give praise for correct observations. If the child is wrong, offer further encouragement to try again. Finally, pass out the paper and pens and ask the child to draw what they hear and discuss their drawings. This is a good activity to do seasonally.

Activity 5: Hanging baskets

Aim

Taking part in a good distracting activity from personal anxieties, instilling a sense of anticipation for the future and learning deferred gratification.

Tools

You will need the following items:

- hanging baskets (ask for donations: many people have spare plastic baskets, which do not require lining, or wire hanging baskets, which will require lining)

- potting soil

- variety of annuals, for example, fuchsia, geraniums, pansies and other trailing plants such as nemesia, which are fragrant and come in many colours.

- watering can

- tape and permanent marker for naming basket (to avoid confusion at the end of school year).

The activity

Prepare a hanging basket containing three plants before-hand as a demonstration basket.

Ensure you have approximately 30 minutes for this activity.

1. Place all the available hanging baskets in a row. If your baskets are made of wire ensure you have lined them prior to the activity.

2. Have the potting soil bag opened and if possible on a table or potting shelf for ease of use.

3. Arrange the plants together in groups of three to give the child a visual clue as to how to select plants and plant up the basket.

4. Lead the child to the garden or potting area and give them freedom of choice to select a basket. Before they get distracted by the plants on offer, ask the child to fill their hanging basket three-quarters full with potting soil.

5. Using the hanging basket you have already prepared as a visual clue, tell the child they can select three plants. Now stand back and mindfully allow yourself to be at ease with their choice of plants. If they decide to pick three plants of the same variety that is fine. Please do not control or judge their choices: this includes managing your facial expression. Remain positive and help the child to plant up the basket by removing the plants from their pots.

6. If you are working in a group, encourage the children to check out each other's hanging baskets as they are building their own, as it is always very reassuring to see other examples when starting an activity.

7. Water the basket.

8. Place the basket in a prominent place in the garden with ease of access for the child to water and deadhead flowers.

9. Ensure you praise each finished basket and tell the child they will get to take the basket home at the end of the school year.

Giving a child their own hanging basket that they will get to take home at the end of the school year and a selection of plants to choose from is a simple but perfect idea. You may be surprised to see how attentive the children are to watering and deadheading their baskets and how much they will bug you about when they get to take their basket home.

Chapter 7

Developmental Disability

Approach

It is key, first and foremost, to consider the strengths of the child you are going to be gardening with. These activities will need to be adapted to ensure success which will result in subsequent increase in self-esteem. Without achievement in these introductory activities, a child's interest for gardening will be dented as they have not felt satisfied enough to be motivated to do more.

Benefits of gardening for children with a developmental disability

This is a wide functioning group in both need and level of ability and therefore activities must be adapted to the individual children. A garden programme has nothing but positive benefits to it. Simply getting outside in the fresh air and sunshine is a benefit so go ahead and try these activities.

The benefits of gardening for children with developmental disability include the following:

- *Physiological:* improved fine and gross motor skills; physical fitness through movement involved in gardening activities such as watering, weeding, digging and walking to obtain garden supplies.

- *Psychological:* increased self-esteem; increased sense of self; redirecting aggressive behaviour.

- *Cognitive:* stimulating curiosity in life sciences and vocabulary; counting; sequences and seasonal changes.
- *Recreational:* age-appropriate leisure skills.
- *Socialization benefits:* opportunity to join community garden clubs and groups.
- *Vocational:* transferable employment skills.

Activities

Be sure to consider the strengths of the child before you begin these activities to anticipate any potential frustration.

Activity 1: Starting a collection

Aim
Using a motivational tool to study and share in context, and encouraging collecting, thus helping to feed the development of classification.

Tools
For this activity you will need:

- garden or nature setting
- empty shoebox, tin with lid or ziplock bag
- hand trowel for digging
- garden gloves
- your imagination.

The activity
If you think back to your childhood we all had a collection, whether it was toys, stamps, bugs, rocks or books. Using nature is an economical way to start a collection and a hugely motivational tool to get outside and stimulate a child's curiosity about the world. I find that rocks, stones and any kind of lumpy concrete found while digging can be highly motivational and I have never met a child who hasn't wanted a rock collection. Ask the child to find some stones (this may involve digging). Below are some interesting facts you can tell the child as you begin your search. Why not get some books out on the British sculptor Andy Goldsworthy to see what can be created with the stones and rocks you collect. This collecting activity encourages initiative, finding, labeling and storing – all important life skills. It teaches that all soil was once rock.

Interesting facts about the earth

The earth is made up of four layers:

- *crust:* ten miles of rock and loose material
- *mantle:* 85 per cent of the earth's weight, super-hot rock
- *outer core:* lava rock, found 3,000 miles beneath the earth's surface
- *inner core:* centre of the earth, made of mostly iron and nickel.

Geologists study the lithosphere. The lithosphere is the surface of the earth. The word 'geo' means 'earth'. Encourage the children to study the characteristics of each rock and make a journal with their observations.

For further exploration of rocks check out the Geology for Kids and Science Kids websites at www.kidsgeo.com/geology-for-kids and www.sciencekids.co.nz/projects.html respectively.

Activity 2: Create a nature busy box

Aim
Stimulating and encouraging new interests, activities and communication by sharing memories.

Tools
For this activity you will need:

- solid box such as a plastic box with airtight lid
- garden or nature setting
- hand trowel for digging
- gloves for touching and collecting items
- some items you have already found as examples, such as interesting shaped rocks, an empty bird nest, snail shells and seed pods.

The activity
Creating a nature busy box is an ideal way to break the ice with a child who is shy or experiencing difficulty making friends. The idea is to fill mini boxes or tins with items that rattle and make noises, which encourages communication. Here are some suggestions:

- stones (a variety)
- drift wood or twigs
- snail shells, crab shells, snake skins and birds' feathers
- dried flowers, seed pods and leaves.

Activity 3: Exploring scents

Aim
Learning through our senses.

Tools
You will need to select a variety of scents:

- calming: lavender and roses
- invigorating: peppermint, lemon
- smells that make us want to taste them: maple syrup, apple, peanut butter, vanilla, chocolate.

The activity
This is a good activity to do either one to one or in a group to encourage social interaction for a group counselling session (as an ice breaker).

1. Allow the child freedom to choose which scent to smell.

2. Make a note of what they like and do not like.

3. Praise the child for sharing scents and waiting politely for turns to smell.

Lavender and roses

Activity 4: Transplanting seedlings

Aim

Observing verbal directions and maintaining focus by following a five-step seedling transplanting process unassisted, three consecutive times.

Tools

You will need the following items:

- seedlings of large plants such as pumpkin or sunflower, 4–5 weeks old
- chopstick, spoon or pencil
- larger pots
- potting soil
- watering can.

The activity

1. Prepare larger individual pots by filling them three-quarters full of potting soil.

2. Using the chopstick, a spoon or a pencil as a dibber, make a hole in the soil in the larger pot.

3. Gently hold the first leaves to appear on the seedling with your fingers and, using a chopstick to dip into the soil to help dislodge the roots of the seedling, pull the seedling out.

4. Place seedling gently into the hole and press soil gently around seedling.

5. Water seedling and place on a bright but not too sunny window sill.

Activity 5: Making lavender shortbread

Aim
An easy and quick recipe which requires reading, measuring and harvesting from the garden.

Tools
You will need the following items:

- cooking bowl and wooden spoon and/or electric mixer
- small rectangular tin, greased (approx. 8" × 8" × 2" or 20 × 20 × 5cm)
- knife
- 220g plain flour
- 2 teaspoons of fresh lavender blooms (no stalks), or 1 teaspoon if dried
- 140g softened unsalted butter
- 70g caster sugar.

The activity
This activity takes approximately ten minutes and the result is great to taste! Be sure to make more than you need as everyone will want to try some when they hear what you're making.

1. Preheat the oven to 350° Farenheit/180° Celsius/ Gas Mark 4.

2. Beat together all the ingredients either by hand or with an electric mixer.

3. Work mixture into a dough and using a fork press evenly into the greased tin.

4. Prick dough with fork.

5. Bake for 20–25 minutes. The shortbread should look light brown when ready.

6. Remove the shortbread from the oven.

7. Using a knife, slowly cut the shortbread into slices while it is warm, and leave to cool.

Enjoy!

Lavender shortbread

Chapter 8

Wheelchair Users

Children in wheelchairs deserve a little more effort and thought on our part to make gardening easy and accessible. The more fuss made, the less comfortable a child will feel. Be prepared, having everything you need to hand, and encourage a buddy to come out to the garden too.

Approach

Christine Pollard, a founding member of the Canadian Horticultural Therapy Association, told me once to concentrate on a person's ability, not their disability, and I carry this with me in my day to day work. It is all too easy to concentrate on a person's weaknesses, not strengths. Through working in the garden we can offer praise and reward to children for their successes and achievements. A key principle of mindfulness practice is being non-judgemental. If a child is displaying feelings of hopelessness and irritability, don't take this personally as a reflection on your skills as an educator or parent. This is a person in pain. Without any strings attached, offer loving kindness in your approach to working with children in pain.

We have to help students adjust to their disability and mobility challenges with compassion and acceptance. Being non-judgemental takes practice and you will have to mentally check yourself. Just becoming aware that you are judging someone is taking the first step in becoming more mindful and should be pleased with yourself for recognizing this. As a mother, I can often be a little over-protective and I know support staff can too. However, I can assure you that you will see a different side to the child you are working with outside given the opportunity.

Take a moment. Consider what it is like to be confined to a wheelchair as a child. All those school water slide trips you can't participate in. You're missing out on opportunities to goof about with your friends and you won't have those silly stories with your peers as the year goes by which are some of our most cherished memories. Not only this, but as well as spinal cord injury you may have other physical and cognitive disabilities such as neurological or visual impairment. You're fed up with questions and people fussing around you asking you how you are so you answer, 'Just fine'. But you're not. Maybe you're in pain all day and you're self-conscious of the wheelchair you're using, you lack motivation and are not keen to participate in social situations.

It's not a great picture is it? Now, imagine a support teacher recognizing the need for something else that the classroom environment just can't offer – taking you outside on a bright sunny day, handing you the garden hose, turning it to jet spray and saying, 'Aim at the parsley!' What a fun way to learn how to identify plants, what a release to be outside. This child may not be able to communicate to you directly, but while aiming water at the plants they will be feeling exhilarated, less frustrated and curious – what is this place? The school garden!

Common barriers to gardening

We need to overcome the following barriers to gardening:

- Gardening may be painful or cause pain.
- The garden isn't safe because we don't know which are the poisonous plants.
- The garden isn't accessible.

- We don't have a garden.

- The weather is prohibitive.

Warm up exercises will help with pain and stiffness. Also, taking regular breaks to enjoy the wonders of nature around us are essential. Have a blanket and hat to hand. Feeling the elements outside, we become more aware of the seasons and feel more alive. If you don't have a school garden, you can select an area that could become home to some containers for planting, maybe even at the front of the school in the entranceway. You will make your principal and colleagues very happy if there are beautiful blooms in pots to greet them every day.

Benefits of gardening for wheelchair users

A garden or nature setting offers children an opportunity to learn more inclusive play without becoming too aware of their own mobility challenges. While initially, we may not be challenging muscles below the level of injury, the benefits to wheelchair users of gardening are many, including the following areas:

- accessible play

- inclusive play

- emotional (creating a positive and curious state of mind)

- self-awareness

- learning in 'context' which is motivating

- increased opportunity to exercise

- opportunities to socialize

- acceptance

- offering distraction

- stress reduction
- redirection of interest
- anticipation of excursions to purchase plants or visit botanical gardens
- improvement of quality of lifestyle
- development of understanding of sequences and patterns
- work capacity and tolerance
- stimulate sensory development
- decision making
- problem solving
- increased self-esteem through mastery and achievement
- increase in verbal and communication skills
- building a sense of outside
- cooperation.

FUNCTIONAL SKILL BENEFITS OF GARDENING

Gardening provides many functional skill benefits, including the following:

- change of dominance (for children with mixed dominance, i.e. eye, hand and foot are not lined up, which may lead to spatial and depth perception issues)
- one-handed techniques
- strengthening use of affected hand
- joint protection
- development of:
  - fine motor skills
  - hand–eye coordination

- ⊛ muscle strength
- ⊛ balance and perception
- ⊛ range of motion
- ⊛ activity tolerance
- ⊛ dynamic sitting
- decreased isolation (opportunity to build new interest and join local garden clubs)
- education about house plant and garden care
- using adaptive techniques.

Hand function and joint protection

Radius tools
Photo courtesy of Lee Valley Tools Ltd

It's important not to overreach or bend at the waist, which means using adaptive tools and working at a bench or raised bed that is customized for wheelchairs. The use of adaptive tools protects joints and eases the pressure on muscles in our hands. Lightweight ergonomic tools such as the Radius® range in the Lee Valley Tools catalogue will allow the strongest arm muscles to do the work, while keeping the joints in their natural positions (see www. leevalley.com). These tools have larger handles too, which allows for an easier grip. Many garden centres now offer a range of ergonomic tools; however, there are some very interesting tools and ideas that you might not find in your local garden centre or hardware store that can really change your lifestyle and I hope you try them.

ADAPTIVE TOOLS

When buying adaptive tools you're looking for tools that are designed for use in the following circumstances:

- sitting down
- using one handed
- needing to use something lightweight
- having difficulty bending, thus avoiding tools that would lead to bending at the waist
- having a weak grip
- being blind or partially sighted, thus needing good grips, bright colours.

Adaptive tools can be used in the following ways:

- Long-handled tools for limited hand and arm movement allow the hands to stay close to the body as opposed to extending the arms out.
- Grips can be added to handles for easier hold (add foam or duct tape if needed).
- Attach Velcro straps around arm and tool, which increases stability and helps with positioning tools for gardening and for easier graft.

- The cut and hold flower gatherer can cut and grip a flower stem, making it easy to deadhead and pick flowers. It is made by A. Wright and Son (supplier's website is at www.penknives-and-scissors.co.uk).

- Easi-grip cultivator, fork and trowel tools; for example, those made by Peta UK Company (www.peta-uk.com) relieve stress on hand and wrist.

- Consider changing door handles and gate latches to levers.

- When buying secateurs (pruning shears), consider buying ratchet action secateurs which require less force. You can also purchase battery operated secateurs for those children with a very limited grip.

- Hi-lo pulleys (e.g. from Lee Valley Tools) can be used for hanging baskets.

- Stainless steel tools and polished aluminium tools are easier to use in soils.

- Use lightweight soil when possible to save energy, and avoid working in heavy clay soil.

If you would like to find further information about adaptive tools, the UK based charity Thrive has an excellent section about adaptive tools and where to buy them on its website, Carry on Gardening (www.carryongardening.org.uk), under the 'Equipment and tools to help you' menu item. In North America try the Disabled Independent Gardeners Association (www.disabilityfoundation.org/diga) and the Tetra Society (www.tetrasociety.org).

WATERING THE GARDEN

Here are some tips for watering the garden:

- Use a trigger-release lance and water-mist lance for watering plants.

- Self-coiling hoses are easier to handle.

- Consider using sprinklers and timed drip irrigation hoses, but if it is feasible, do water by hand as it's a relaxing activity and I know many children find this one of the most enjoyable parts of their day.

- Turn the hose on to jet spray and ask the child to aim for the plants you name. This is a fun way to learn to identify plants.

I find that watering the garden is a good motivator to get basic jobs such as weeding done first. It works every time but be prepared to get a bit wet even if you think you're paying attention. Sometimes life just throws situations at you that there is no way you can be prepared for. It's inevitable. For example, I recently was asked to hold an earthworm one child found. At the same time the worm was delivered into my hand, another child watering thought it would be nice to give the worm a squirt of water from the hose to clean it off. I got a big, fat, juicy earthworm, soil and water all blown into my face. At such a moment stop, check yourself and remain calm. Both the earthworm and I survived to see another day. Who do you think the children were more concerned about?

Designing a nature play and exploration garden

Raised bed for wheelchair users

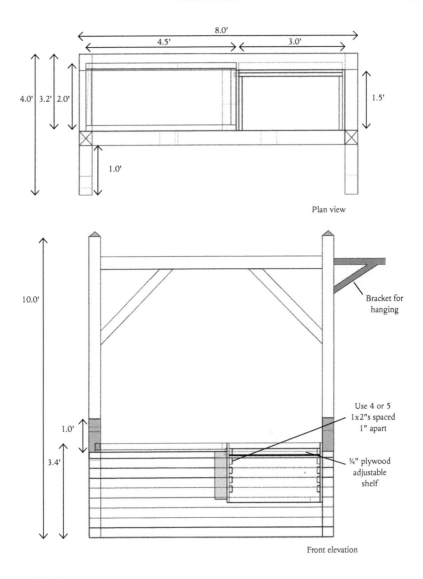

8.0'
4.5'
3.0'
4.0' 3.2' 2.0'
1.5'
1.0'

Plan view

10.0'

Bracket for hanging

Use 4 or 5
1x2"s spaced
1" apart

1.0'

¾" plywood
adjustable
shelf

3.4'

Front elevation

Dimensions for enabling garden
Designed by Natasha Etherington (Horticultural Therapist), constructed by
Steve Hodgins, drawing by Dolores Altin. (Note: all dimensions are approx.)

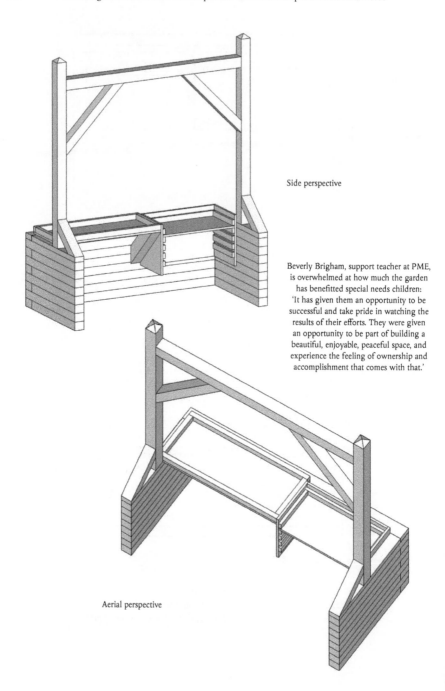

Side perspective

Beverly Brigham, support teacher at PME, is overwhelmed at how much the garden has benefitted special needs children: 'It has given them an opportunity to be successful and take pride in watching the results of their efforts. They were given an opportunity to be part of building a beautiful, enjoyable, peaceful space, and experience the feeling of ownership and accomplishment that comes with that.'

Aerial perspective

I think good designs work best when the designer has a very thorough understanding of the need and function required. I customized a regular A frame raised bed in a school garden for a wheelchair user. The A frame was inset into the garden border (to avoid being knocked by other students) with a 4 inch high shelf protruding 2 feet in depth (see sketch for dimensions). This was to enable the student to approach the bed straight on and to place their hand on the electric controls without scraping any skin on the cedar. No adaptive tools were necessary as the enabling garden was customized to work for a particular sized wheelchair. Beside is an adjustable potting shelf which a support worker or buddy can work at nearby without getting too close. The adjustable potting shelf enables a variety of wheelchairs users to work at it. Either side are hanging baskets adjustable from beneath with hi-lo pulleys, which enable the gardener to push them up from underneath to release them. It is preferable to use the least amount of energy possible getting to the garden, so hanging baskets are a good option if getting outside is proving difficult or the weather prohibitive as they can be worked on indoors.

It is best to avoid having raised beds that may scrape a wheelchair user's hands or arms or involve having to twist to garden in, so keep this in mind when constructing raised beds. Although encouraging flexibility is key, I don't think anyone in a wheelchair should have to twist for long periods while gardening.

In a nature play and exploration garden, many elements can help to engage children:

- sensory garden with plants to smell, touch, taste and work in (see Appendix 4 for sensory plant suggestions)
- digging plot for exploration and educating about the importance of soil

- a snoozle lawn for increased movement, crawling and rolling (see p.113)

- other areas for exploration and discovery (take a step back and think simple: objects to collect such as rocks or a log that an animal has chewed on are fascinating to children) and keep tools nearby for ease of use

- manipulative materials

- wide paths (at least 5 feet or 1.5 metres)

- deciduous trees (those that drop their leaves each autumn, such as fruit trees) to highlight seasons with plant material (leaves and seed pods)

- water play: water fascinates children and water play can be used to enhance understanding of mathematical concepts, fine motor skills and vocabulary

- features that develop motor skills, places to climb through and balance

- places for make-believe play, for groups and social places such as a storytelling area (this might be just a boulder in a shady corner for a teacher to sit on, a grass area for children to relax on or a teepee made out of sticks)

- areas for cooperative play (such as a sand pit)

- spaces for moving, climbing and throwing

- a water feature or wind chimes as audible signposts to aid navigation of the garden for visually impaired children.

All gardening activities such as watering plants, weeding, propagating with cuttings and pruning plants are achievable for wheelchair users. It is important to note, however, that a frustrating activity will really put a child off quickly.

Building up gradual increases in physical challenge is ideal. Be sure to point out successes and create a fun environment with sensory plant material. As Christopher Reeve[1] pointed out, 'Nothing is impossible.'

Warm up exercises

It's important to warm up muscles prior to gardening and to become aware if a particular joint is aching while we work. If aching or pain do occur, it is time to stop and take a break. Do not garden for more than one hour at a time with a child.

Here are some examples of warm up stretches you may want to make part of your outdoor routine:

- *Wrist stretch 1:* make circles with each fist, first one way, then the other. Bend each wrist up and bend it down.

- *Wrist stretch 2:* put palms together and fingers together, then hold arms stretched out together in front. Pull your hands in toward chest and repeat a few times.

- *Shoulder stretch:* bring arms together in front of you with elbows touching, then widen your arms to either side of your body with your hands up in the air. Now stretch arms overhead as far as possible, keeping your elbows in line with the side of your body.

- *Finger and thumb stretch:* place hands on table with fingers pointing ahead. Slide thumbs towards each other. Slide each finger one at a time toward the thumb as if your fingers are walking. Then lay your fingers down straight. Hold hand in front of you with thumb

---

1   Inspirational actor and founder of the Reeve Foundation, which is dedicated to curing spinal cord injury and the improving quality of life for people living with paralysis.

pointing up. Move thumb in large circular movements in each direction.

For further information on gardening for people with disabilities and accessible play spaces, I recommend checking out the following websites: Thrive (www.thrive.org.uk), Rick Hansen (www.rickhansen.com) and the Reeve Foundation (www.christopherreeve.org). See also the Recommended Resources section.

Activities

It is ideal if teachers and parents work together and learn together in the garden through these activities.

Activity 1: Gaining a sense of outside

Aim

This activity is a cognitive, physical and sensory stimulant. Take this opportunity to do stretches and deep breathing exercises, becoming fully present in nature.

Tools

You will need the following items:

- blanket
- hat
- sunscreen
- water spray
- herbs to touch, crush, taste and smell.

The activity

This activity may seem obvious but if you try to remember the last time you went outside and did nothing, absolutely nothing, I bet it was a long time ago. This activity will really help reset the mood of the child and decrease anxiety.

1. Ensure the child is comfortable and have a hat or blanket to hand if the weather changes.

2. Encourage and help the child to move from the wheelchair and sit on a bench or preferably a grass area.

3. Observe the weather. Can you see any trees? Just sit and listen. What noises do you hear? Observe the beauty of nature.

4. Let the child take the lead. Do they want to roll or crawl towards a plant?

5. Watch their focus.

6. Make a note of what stimulates the child. It may be a bird arriving on a branch nearby or a bee flying by.

7. Introduce a herb for the child to touch, crush, taste and smell. This will help with associating with the outside.

8. If you're with a child with visual impairment and low mobility, perhaps lightly spray their face with water (with parental permission) to stimulate their senses and to help them gain a true sense of being outside. The wind is wonderful and energizing, as is a beautiful sunbeam to re-energize in. I feel most alive myself on a really windy day. It blows all our worries and cares away.

9. Take this time to ask the child to stretch. Do some neck stretches, shrug shoulder stretches and full body stretches. Rest in these poses and feel the earth beneath you. Add in some large deep breaths to aid relaxation and really feel the benefit of Mother Earth (see also Appendix 6). Are there any trees nearby? They are producing oxygen as a by-product of photosynthesis, helping us to breathe and protecting us with shade from the heat of the sun. Maybe there are some fruit trees nearby? Touch, feel and taste if the fruit is edible.

Activity 2: A snoozle lawn

Aim

Promoting positive associations for mind and body combined with getting outside and exercise.

Tools

You will need the following items:

- grass area, preferably sloped to encourage movement and crawling: look for an area that has trees around it so that when you lie back on the grass there are branches overhead to give you a feeling of security

- a hand water spray

- a bird feeder

- herbs such as lemon balm, parsley or whatever you have nearby.

Snoozle lawn

The activity

At Pitt Meadows Elementary we have a snoozle lawn I built for a child with cerebral palsy. This is a multisensory lawn raised at 1ft (30cm) to enable the support team to transfer the child from the wheelchair onto the grass with ease. The lawn slopes upwards with a slight gradient to encourage movement and crawling. The lawn is small, 10ft by 16ft (3m by 5m); however, this is large enough for a whole class to fit on for story time and art classes. I leave a chair beside the lawn so that teachers don't have to worry about worms or grass stains on their clothes. Around the lawn are ornamental grasses and edible plants such as a blueberry. I'd suggest not planting too much lavender around an area where a child with low mobility is resting, as lavender does attract bees (only really a problem in the summer). My biggest challenge with the lawn to date has been preventing it from being mowed. Long grass is stimulating for our senses and many children don't get the opportunity to play in long grass. In addition, leaving the grass long will help the grass survive the summer heat as it may burn on top but will spring back the next year.

Benefits of having a grass area in your garden

- Grass has therapeutic value in helping to decrease blood pressure and anxieties.

- Grass is pleasing to the eye.

- Grass is soft and thus safe.

- Green grass contrasts with the harshness of concrete walls and glass.

- Grass has a multisensory use. Encourage children to remove their shoes and socks and to really feel the grass. Is it tickly? Does it smell like they think grass should smell?

- Long grass helps with conservation. It provides a place for insects and other invertebrates to roam.

- Insects and worms provide a source of food for birds.

- Nothing is quite as exciting as a spontaneous visit by a bird to an overhead bird feeder.

Activity 3: Introduction to soil

Aim

Introducing soil, understanding what soil is and how plants need the right conditions for growing, and stimulating the senses.

Tools

You will need the following items:

- lightweight sterilized soil (potting soil is fine)
- large container or deep tray if no access to a raised bed or enabling garden
- gallon container of sand (could be play sand as it's the texture you need)
- gallon container of clay (ask around to find out if anyone you know has clay soil in their garden, or try a riverbank as some rivers have clay banks).

The activity

1. Place Rubbermaid or other deep tray on the child's lap.
2. Pour sand in the tray.
3. Gently place the child's hands in the sand.
4. Spread their fingers and hold them in the sand for a short while.
5. By gently squeezing the handfuls of sand and releasing, we're warming up our hand muscles. Repeat this a few times.

6. Then repeat this exercise with clay and then the potting soil.

If working with hands is not possible, use the child's feet. This is a multisensory introductory gardening activity which incorporates warm up exercises for hand muscles. Smelling and touching the sand, clay and soil is really going to stimulate our senses. The *Vancouver Sun* (2010) newspaper reported that Dr Dorothy Matthews, an associate professor of biology at the Sage Colleges of Troy, NY, stated that soil releases bacteria which produces serotonin in our bodies. By getting outside we're exposing ourselves to mycobacterium vaccae – a natural soil microbe which enhances the release of serotonin which is a mood adjuster. By working in soil we're making ourselves happy. Dr Matthews recommended that time be made in schools for children to learn outdoors, which may decrease their anxiety and improve their ability to learn new tasks. I couldn't agree more.

An ideal loam soil for planting contains a balance of sand, silt and clay and organic material (plus air and water). Loam soil also has a balance of micro and macro pores in it for holding nutrients. Soil is fascinating and home to millions of micro-organisms. Read Chapter 3, 'Why Dig?', for more information on soil.

Activity 4: Sowing seeds

Aim
A multisensory introductory gardening activity which develops fine motor skills and sequencing.

Tools
You will need the following items:

- large seeds such as sunflower seeds, pumpkin seeds or beans (work your way to smaller seeds such as radish, lettuce and marigolds next)
- potting soil
- empty cardboard toilet rolls, rolled up newspaper or other biodegradable pots
- watering can
- plastic ziplock bags
- tray or potting bench.

The activity
Don't throw away the seed packet instructions: keep them for reference. You may have to get creative to adapt to each child's disability. Any preparation you have made beforehand to enable them to do this activity will be much appreciated.

1. Fill pots with potting soil, leaving 1 or 2 inches at the top.

2. Squeeze and smell the soil. What's in the soil? There may be perlite, which is used to improve germination and aeration.

3. Take a look at the seeds. A seed has a seed coat which is hard.

4. Drop one or two seeds into the pot of soil. If this is difficult, use an empty toilet roll to drop the seeds down as a chute into the pot. Then layer about 1–2 inches of soil on top. Ensure you read the instructions on the seed packet to find out the depth at which the seed should be planted – some seeds are surface sowed and others need to be placed beneath the soil.

5. Using a watering can, sprinkle the pots with water to moisten the soil.

6. Cover the pots with a plastic translucent ziplock bag to create a mini greenhouse effect.

7. Once you start to see seedlings sprouting, remove the plastic bags so they do not stunt the growth of the seedling.

8. When the seedlings are ready to be transplanted outside, dig a hole the depth of the pot and pop the whole pot into the garden bed.

9. The pot will degrade by itself in the soil over time. This makes transplanting seedlings much easier and there is less chance of plants being squashed and roots damaged.

In addition to using pots, you can sow sunflower seeds directly in the garden bed from the end of March, or start off indoors from February.

Sow pumpkin seeds or beans directly in the garden bed from May onwards or start indoors in April in pots.

I would recommend starting sowing seeds indoors as this activity stimulates our curiosity and provides a big sense of achievement upon completion. This might also be a good activity to encourage some lifting, for example when pouring the soil, watering or moving completed pots to a tray. Try to take a step back, mentally check and stop yourself passing items when the child could reach and lift the tools they need themselves. They will be so engrossed in the activity they may not even realize what they've achieved. Be mindful; write down what you see so you don't forget later on to point out their successes. Encourage them to do more.

Please note if you started your seedlings off in plastic starter pots, you will need to remove the seedlings from the pots. The best way to do this is to hold the top leaves and use a chopstick, dibber or pencil to ease the plant out carefully and place it into the garden bed. Do not worry too much if you tear a leaf: the plant should still grow. It's more important to try to keep the root intact while transplanting.

Finally, ask the child how they feel about sowing the seeds and check to see whether they understand how long germination (seedling sprouting) may take. This will be on the back of the seed packet. You may want to mark this off on a calendar and encourage a garden journal to be kept. Next you might want to try smaller seeds. You could also consider planting some crocus or daffodil bulbs in the autumn for something to look forward to in the spring.

Sowing seeds is an essential component of becoming a gardener and gives us something to look forward to nurturing. If purchasing seeds is difficult, ask your parent advisory board for some money to purchase seeds for your gardening scheme or ask for seed donations in your school newsletter. Local hardware stores are also happy to provide school donations. A garden is a great way to make new contacts and I'd be surprised if there isn't a parent at your school who doesn't work in the horticultural trade. I also find most garden centres only too willing to give away free pots and containers.

Chapter 9

Poisonous Plants

In this chapter I will concentrate on those plants most commonly planted in schools and associated with children. It is important that you learn the identity of each plant that the child is going to come in contact with. For example, a popular autumnal plant such as the Chinese lantern, also known as ground cherry or winter cherry (*Physalis alkekengi*), has poisonous parts which may cause stomach ache if eaten and contact with the foliage may cause skin irritation. Only the ripe fruit is edible.

Toxicity

The term toxic means unsafe. There are four classes of toxicity in plants, as follows:

- *Major toxicity:* these plants cause serious illness or death. If ingested you must go to hospital straight away.

- *Minor toxicity:* ingestion of these plants may cause minor illness such as vomiting or diarrhoea.

- *Oxalates:* the juice of the sap of these plants contains oxalate crystals. These needle-shaped crystals can irritate the skin, mouth, tongue and throat, resulting in pain and breathing difficulties.

- *Dermatitis:* the juice, sap or thorns of these plants may cause a skin rash or irritation. Wash the affected area of skin with soap and water as soon as possible after contact.

TOP TEN TOXIC (UNSAFE) PLANTS

Many teachers and parents are surprised to know that the following plants are toxic:

- foxgloves: all parts poisonous

- lupins: all parts poisonous

- rhubarb: leaves but not stem

- common English ivy, Boston ivy and other varieties: leaves are poisonous.

- castor bean and castor oil plant: seeds are very toxic

- oleander (ornamental shrub): all parts are highly toxic

- tomato: leaves can be an irritant

- poinsettia: latex (the milky sap exuded by some plants), leaves and stem are poisonous

- chrysanthemum: leaves and stalks are poisonous and can cause contact dermatitis

- some members of the daisy family (*Asteraceae*): leading cause of contact dermatitis in florists (do not fear the common lawn daisy *Bellis perennis*).

While foxgloves and lupins are beautiful plants and a great source of nectar for beneficial insects, it's far better to remove all toxic plants from a garden that children with special needs will visit. Most children would agree that learning to identify toxic plants is important. Consider planning a nature walk where you can point out toxic plants such as foxgloves to children. I would recommend never tasting a plant without adult supervision.

TOXIC AND NON-TOXIC HOUSE PLANTS

Three of the most common toxic (unsafe) houseplants are:

- philodendron
- ivy
- croton.

There are a number of non-toxic (safe) houseplants:

- jade plant
- palm
- ferns
- spider plant
- wandering Jew
- violets
- Boston fern
- bromeliads
- Christmas cactus.

Phototoxic plants

If you're working with a child who is on medication and/or has sensitive skin, you should know that there are some plants you should not work with in full sun. The sun can cause a dermatotoxic action which is called phytophotodermatitis (dermatitis due to plants and light).

The most common causes occur in the Umbelliferae family (the carrot family sometimes called the Apiaceae) and citrus species of the Rutaceae family.

Common phototoxic plants include the following:

- globe thistle
- fig

- dill

- celery

- lime

- lemon

- grapefruit

- French marigolds

- parsley

- euphorbia.

Finally, if you're faced with a huge area covered in weeds and plants that you're not sure of the identity, bring in some goats. Goats have cast iron stomachs and can digest what most cattle cannot.

For further information, a good resource is the Washington Poison Center (www.wapc.org), which is a non-profit organization with comprehensive lists of non-toxic and toxic plants. In the United Kingdom contact NHS Direct (www.nhsdirect.nhs.uk). In Canada go to British Columbia Drug and Poison Information Service (www.dpic.org) and read http://dpic.org/sites/default/files/pdf/PlantAwareness2007.pdf.

Chapter 10

Gardens for Children who Suffer from Asthma and Allergies

I find pollen fascinating. The subject deserves a book in its own right to capture children's attention. Pollen is the powdery substance produced by the male part of a flower, which contains the fertilizing agent for the female's seeds. If a plant is pollinated by an insect, it means that a bee, for example, has landed on the flower to drink nectar from the plant and in so doing inadvertently rubs the pollen onto its back. As it flies around visiting plants it will inevitably visit a female plant thus rubbing the pollen onto the stigma (female part) and fertilizing the plants' eggs ready to produce seeds.

Unfortunately, many parents are put off visiting gardens and parks for fear that some plants' pollen (plants unidentifiable to them) will trigger allergic reactions in their children. Through educating ourselves we can dispel the myths regarding allergenic reactions. You have my full sympathy if you care for a child with allergies, as my husband suffers with allergies himself. It doesn't mean he can't climb trees or enjoy the aesthetic beauty of gardens or plants, but unfortunately, he will never truly enjoy the fragrance of a flower. It is the most fragrant plants that often trigger allergies in children and adults alike. The Asteraceae family (asters and daisies) is by far the largest family of plants that produce allergenic pollen.

There are two types of pollen that plants produce:

- pollen carried by the wind
- pollen carried by beneficial insects and birds.

Pollen carried in the air by the wind is an airborne allergen. The most common allergy caused by pollen is hay fever (allergic rhinitis). It's not just pollen that can trigger asthma attacks. For example, western red cedar sawdust (*Thuju plicata*) is a common trigger in the Pacific North West. Many weeds such as stinging nettles, plantain and ragweed are all wind pollinated. Ragweed in the Pacific North West is particularly irritant to allergenic sufferers.

Plants to use

Here are some examples of plants to use if your child has allergic rhinitis; they are pollinated by beneficial insects and birds.

Herbaceous perennials (plants that live for several years) include the following:

- hostas
- sedges (instead of ornamental grasses)
- Siberian iris (*Iris sibirica*)
- astilbe
- Japanese anemone (*Anemone x* hybrid).

Annuals and biennials include the following:

- snapdragon (*Antirrhinum majus*)
- bacopa
- black-eyed Susan (*Rudbeckia hirta*)
- nasturtium (*Tropaeolum*).

Herbs include the following:

- chives
- fennel
- lemon balm
- mint
- basil
- sage
- parsley
- thyme.

Shrubs include the following:

- Russian sage (*Perovskia atriplicifolia*)
- peony (*Paeonia delavayi*)
- broom (*Genista lydia*)
- dogwood (*Cornus alba*)
- smoke bush (*Cotinus goggygria*).

Hedging includes the following:

- garden thyme (*Thymus vulgaris*): all thyme is attractive to bees
- rhododendrons and azaleas.

In the Pacific North West rhododendrons and azaleas often provide the background planting for a border with evergreen interest. Their lush leaves and beautiful range of flower colours and shapes are good for attracting a variety of beneficial insects. They also do not mind the shade.

Groundcover plants include the following:

- winter flowering heather (*Erica carnea*)
- lady's mantle (*Alchemilla mollis*)

- speedwell (*Veronica*)
- fuchsia.

Trees include the following:

- winter-flowering cherry (*Prunus x subhirtella 'Autumnalis'*): this does attract bees so avoid if allergic to bee stings
- kowhai (*Stewartia pseudocamellia*): this has all season interest with peeling bark and rose-like flowers.

Plants to avoid

Here are some examples of plants to avoid if your child has allergic rhinitis; they are wind pollinated. Annuals and biennials include the following:

- sunflower (*Helianthus annuus*)
- marigold (*Calendula officinalis*)
- daisy (*Asteraceae* family)
- cornflower (*Centaurea cyanus*)
- sweet pea (*Lathyrus odoratus*)
- tobacco plant (*Nicotiana*)
- osteospermum
- zinnia.

Trees include the following:

- hazel
- red alder
- poplar and aspen
- sycamore
- ash

- plane
- birch
- oak
- maple.

Shrubs include the following:

- wisteria (plant a hardy climbing clematis instead)
- lupins
- box
- lavender
- grasses
- laburnums
- white flowered jasmines (use yellow winter-flowering jasmine)
- Japanese honeysuckle (instead use hardy honeysuckle with no scent).

Vegetables include the following:

- spinach
- sea kale
- beetroot
- sweet corn
- asparagus
- celery
- tomatoes.

Finally, adding gravel to the top of planted up pots will help retain moisture and contain any fungal spores in the soil.

Chapter 11

Conclusion

Gardening books can be overwhelming and therefore I hope that this book will succeed in removing any apprehension you may have and, whatever the weather, get you gardening immediately. Like a well-used cook book, it should become muddied and crinkly from a bit of earth and rain by the end of the growing season.

If there were just three things I hope you remember after reading this book they would be:

1. Getting outside calms our mind and is good for our mind and body.

2. When working with children remain flexible and always, always maintain a sense of humour.

3. Never give up on your unique child and always aim high for them.

I wish you and your child peace and happiness.

Learning Assessment Principles and Learning Goals

Standard learning assessment principles for teachers

The standard learning assessment principles are as follows:

- providing effective feedback to students
- actively involving students in their own learning
- adjusting teaching to take account of the results of assessment
- recognizing the profound influence assessment has on the motivation and self-esteem of pupils, both of which are crucial influences on learning
- ensuring that students are able to assess themselves and understand how to improve.

Individual Education Plan learning goals for support teachers and therapists

Goals to help a child learn in a garden setting include the following:

- Increasing social skills and forming friendships:
  - Goal: to reduce the child's demanding behaviour.
  - Objective: child will ask for tools politely once every session.
- Learning to adapt to unique way of learning:
  - Goal: to increase the child's self-esteem.

⊚ Objective: child will successfully complete one task per session.

- Facilitating ongoing self-assessment both verbal and written by student in a journal:

  ⊚ Goal: to connect the child's feelings and emotions.

  ⊚ Objective: at the end of each gardening session the child will either draw a face with appropriate emotion (happy, sad, anxious) or verbally express feelings so they may be documented.

- Reducing feelings of anxiety and enhancing sense of control:

  ⊚ Goal: to enable the child to accept responsibility.

  ⊚ Objective: the child will weed, water and care for a specific part of the garden for one month.

- Helping to develop an interest in learning and reading:

  ⊚ Goal: to motivate the child's interest in finding information.

  ⊚ Objective: the child will select a plant and care for it daily for one month.

Risk Assessment

A risk assessment should be completed prior to the start of activities. This example will draw your attention to the top ten potential hazards in a garden or nature setting. It is imperative that a special needs student is not left alone in a garden. Make sure that everyone's hands are washed following each activity, particularly prior to eating.

The top ten risks in the garden are discussed below.

Plants

If working with children with sensitive skin, use protective gloves. Any plant substance has the potential to cause an allergic reaction in some people, so use due caution. *Know your plant*: always research the plant you are planning to work with. Only work with non-toxic (safe) plants. Students should not eat plants unless instructed to do so by a responsible adult. Wash hands at the end of gardening. See Chapter 9 on 'Poisonous Plants'.

Soil irritation

Ensure students have up-to-date tetanus inoculation. Ensure there is no access to soil by animals such as cats and dogs (risk of toxoplasmosis). Students with a suppressed immune system and with cuts or abrasions on hands should wear gloves. Moisten dry potting soil before using to avoid it blowing in the wind.

Chemicals

Please be organic! Avoid use of chemicals which will poison plants and children, either through inhalation or skin contact.

Tools

Correct tools are only to be used as instructed by a responsible adult. Ensure sufficient supervision when working with students with severe behavioral difficulties. When working with shovels, ensure adequate space between students. Do not lift tools above shoulder height. Do not run in the garden with tools. Ensure tools are put away at the end of each activity.

Infections

Infections from cuts or abrasions can be prevented by using an antiseptic cream after washing the hands. Children with existing cuts should always use gloves.

Lifting injuries

Injuries can occur when lifting heavy objects such as heavy plants and plant pots. Try to do this in pairs, or use a dollie or wheelbarrow to help you. Ask for volunteers. Try to remember to bend at the knees when lifting objects.

Fallen leaves

Do not run in the garden. Wear gloves if picking up fallen leaves.

Injuries to eyes and face

When using plant supports, place a plastic bottle or yoghurt pot on the top of the support so it is easier to avoid. You can also purchase cane-toppers from most garden centres.

Water

All hoses should be tidied up after use. Do not leave hoses crossing pathways. No running in the garden. If installing water butts, ensure they are securely locked and approved with school administration.

Weather

Always have to hand a variety of hats, caps, blankets and gloves. Umbrellas may also be useful. Students should bring sunscreen spray. In any weather do not run in the garden.

Benefits of Horticultural Therapy and Therapeutic Gardens

The American Horticultural Therapy Association (AHTA 2007) has published a position paper listing benefits of horticultural therapy.

Cognitive benefits

Enhance cognitive functioning (Kaplan and Kaplan, 1989; Cimprich, 1993; Herzog, Black, Fountaine and Knotts, 1997)

Improve concentration (Wells, 2000; Taylor *et al.*, 2001)

Stimulate memory (Namazi and Haynes, 1994)

Improve goal achievement (Willets and Sperling, 1983)

Improve attentional capacity (Hartig, Mang and Evans, 1991; Ulrich *et al.*, 1991; Ulrich and Parsons, 1992; Ulrich, 1999; Taylor *et al.*, 2001)

Psychological benefits

Improve quality of life (Willets and Sperling, 1983; Waliczek *et al.*, 1996)

Increase self-esteem (Moore, 1989; Blair *et al.*, 1991; Smith and Aldous, 1994; Feenstra *et al.*, 1999; Pothukuchi and Bickes, 2001)

Improve sense of well-being (Relf *et al.*, 1992; Ulrich and Parsons, 1992; Galindo and Rodrieguez, 2000; Kaplan, 2001; Jarrott, Kwack and Relf, 2002; Barnicle and Stoelzle Midden, 2003; Hartig, 2003)

Reduce stress (Ulrich and Parsons, 1992; Whitehouse *et al.*, 2001; Rodiek, 2002)

Improve mood (Wichrowski, Whiteson, Haas, Mola and Rey, 2005; Whitehouse *et al.*, 2001)

Decrease anxiety (Mooney and Milstein, 1994)

Alleviate depression (Relf, 1978; Mooney and Milstein, 1994; Cooper Marcus and Barnes, 1999)

Increase sense of control (Relf *et al.*, 1992)

Improve sense of personal worth (Smith and Aldous, 1994)

Increase feelings of calm and relaxation (Moore, 1989; Relf *et al.*, 1992)

Increase sense of stability (Blair *et al.*, 1991; Feenstra *et al.*, 1999; Pothukuchi and Bickes, 2001)

Improve personal satisfaction (Blair *et al.*, 1991; Smith and Aldous, 1994; Feenstra *et al.*, 1999; Pothukuchi and Bickes, 2001)

Increase sense of pride and accomplishment (Hill and Relf, 1982; Matsuo, 1995)

Social benefits

Improve social integration (Kweon, Sullivan and Wiley, 1998)

Increase social interaction (Langer and Rodin, 1976; Moore, 1989; Perrins-Margalis, Rugletic, Schepis, Stepanski and Walsh, 2000)

Provide for healthier patterns of social functioning (Langer and Rodin, 1976; Kuo, Bacaicoa and Sullivan, 1998)

Improved group cohesiveness (Bunn, 1986)

Physical benefits

Improve immune response (Hartig, Mang and Evans, 1991; Ulrich *et al.*, 1991; Ulrich and Parsons, 1992; Ulrich, 1999)

Decrease stress (Rodiek, 2002)

Decrease heart rate (Wichrowski, Whiteson, Haas, Mola and Rey, 2005)

Promote physical health (Ulrich and Parsons, 1992; Kweon, Sullivan and Wiley, 1998; Cooper Marcus and Barnes, 1999; Armstrong, 2000; Rodiek, 2002)

Improve fine and gross motor skills and eye–hand coordination (Moore, 1989)

People and facilities benefiting from horticultural therapy and therapeutic gardens

People of all ages and special needs can benefit from involvement in horticultural therapy. Programs operate throughout the United States as well as in other countries and can be found in the following facility and program types:

Vocational, pre-vocational, occupational and rehabilitation programs

Psychiatric hospitals and mental health programs

Substance abuse programs

Hospitals, clinics, and skilled nursing facilities

Hospice and palliative care programs

Cancer centers

Correctional facilities

Shelters for the homeless and victims of abuse

Public and private schools

Assisted living and senior centers

Adult day care

Community and botanic gardens

Top Ten Sensory Plants, Must Have Herbs and Top Three Oddballs

Top ten multisensory plant suggestions

Here are the top ten sensory plants to interest children and young people.

SUNFLOWERS (*HELIANTHUS ANNUUS*)

The value of sunflowers includes their edible seeds, a source of food for birds. Why not have a sunflower growing competition: their beautiful bright large flower heads brighten up everyone's day. They are easy to grow and will do best with added compost or manure dug into soil. A great plant to study, it has over 1000 flowers. The leaves and buds of young sunflowers exhibit heliotropism, which means their orientation changes from east to west during the course of a day, turning towards the sun.

LAMB'S EAR (*STACHYS BYZANTINA*)

The value of lamb's ear is that it is an evergreen plant that flowers in late spring and early summer. Leaf texture is white, soft and furry. It is easy to grow in partial shade.

ROSES

There is a very wide variety of roses, which have given rise to a wealth of folklore, poetry and literature. Dry the fragrant petals for potpourri activities in the winter; also the flower heads can be hung and dried. Rose hips are high in vitamin C.

POT MARIGOLDS (*CALENDULA OFFICINALIS*)

Marigolds are bright, cheerful and fragrant flowers. The common marigold (*Tagetes*) is a good companion plant in a vegetable patch. It has edible flowers and its fragrance deters pests. Please note it can be invasive in some regions.

SNAPDRAGONS (*ANTIRRHINUM*)

Snapdragons have beautiful flowers in white, crimson and yellow colours. They are fun to play with (add to a fairy theme garden). Squeeze the flowers to make them resemble a dragon snapping its jaws.

CHERRY TOMATOES

Cherry tomatoes are quick to ripen, sweet to taste and bite size, which is easier for children with sensory sensitiveness. Try varieties Jolly Elf and Sweet Baby Girl. In the UK try Tumbling Tiger and Gardener's Delight cherry tomatoes.

GRAPE HYACINTH (*MUSCARI*)

Grape hyacinth are small yet beautiful bright blue urn-shaped flowers resembling tiny bunches of grapes that flower in early spring. These look fantastic in a container under a dwarf azalea or under a deciduous tree. The fragrance is astonishing and invigorating on a cold spring day. These are good value plants as they multiply quickly (naturalize). As with all bulbs they are toxic, so do not eat them. The dried seed heads are fun to collect seeds from and are ready for collecting before the end of the school year.

HYACINTH (*HYACINTHUS ORIENTALIS*)

Force a fragrant hyacinth on a window sill over winter. The hyacinth's fragrance will instil a sense of cheerfulness and anticipation for spring.

Please note the hyacinth bulb contains oxalic acid, which can cause mild irritation. If working with people with sensitive skin, use protective gloves to avoid irritation. If you think the smell may be too overpowering, try forcing a tulip instead such as the dwarf variety Little Red Riding Hood.

PUMPKIN

Pumpkins are edible and their large seeds are easy to work with. It can be used in education for good nutrition and in storytelling, for example Cinderella. Sow pumpkin seeds before the end of school break for when you come back in the autumn. Save the seeds for the following year and make pumpkin pie with the flesh. There are many varieties to try from. Try variety Rouge Vif d'Etamps, an old French heirloom also known as Cinderella and Jack Of All Trades.

SWEET PEAS (*LATHYRUS ODORATUS*)

Sweet peas are known as 'the queen of annuals' and no garden should be without them. Their fragrance is described as a blend of honey and orange blossom and there is a large palette of colours available. Please note that the plant parts, including the seeds, should not be eaten. As it is a climber, consider growing sweet peas up a tepee made out of sticks. Sweet peas make excellent cutting flowers. Try the variety *Fragrantissima* and the heirloom variety Old Spice Blend.

Must have herbs

Must have herbs include the following: lavender, parsley (many varieties including chocolate!), santolina (cotton lavender), lemon balm, curry plant, basil, lovage, marjoram, oregano, rosemary, bergamot, garlic, fernleaf dill, thyme, sage and mint. It is best to grow mint and lemon balm in containers sunk in the border as they are invasive.

Top three oddballs

The first oddball is parasitic plants, such as mistletoe and dodder, which take their food from other living plants. Second, there are insect eating plants such as venus fly trap (*Dionaea muscipula*) and the sundew plant (*Drosera*). Third, there is the fungi kingdom, which is separate from the plant kingdom (not many people know that). Fungi survive on dead and decaying vegetation such as a rotting tree trunk. Buy some mushrooms from your local supermarket and consider using some recipes to cook them. There are over 100,000 species and fungi live all over the world in a variety of habitats.

Themed Containers and Gardens

Video gamer theme container

If you've ever played a video game you'll know how bright and vibrant the plants are. There may also be some carnivorous plants (see the carnivorous plant container below) which might eat the characters you place in the garden, such as the ones that come free with burgers or are bought as part of a collection. Plants I would suggest to use are some of the most showy flowers such as sunflowers, lilies, carnations, rudbeckias and venus fly traps.

Pizza garden container

Grow some basil, cherry tomatoes, chives and even peppers!

Animal garden

Plants with animal names include catmint (*Nepeta cataria*), dogwood (*Cornus alba*), snapdragons (*Antirrhinum*), hens and chicks (*Sempervivum*), butterfly plant (grows and spreads quickly: *Buddleia davidii*), lamb's ear (*Stachys byzantina*: lamb's ears varieties include 'Primrose Heron' and 'Big Ears'), Elephant Ears Begenia, toad lily (*Tricyrtis*) and deer fern (*Blechnum spicant*). Remember that foxgloves are toxic plants.

Flower fairy garden

Use marigold, lavender, sweet pea, poppy, candytuft, tulip and forget-me-nots. Plants with fairy names include Fairy Tale roses, 'Fairy Earrings' fuchsia, 'fairy' snapdragons and 'elfin' thyme.

Consider planting a fairy ring of daffodils or a more traditional mushroom circle.

Space container

Suitable plants include moonflower (*Ipomoea alba*), venus fly trap (*Dionaea muscipula*), rocket (*Eruca sativa*), cosmos and Jupiter's beard (*Centranthus rubber*).

Christmas container

You could use lingon berry (*Vaccinium vitis-idaea*), evergreen boughs such as cedar and laurel, and Christmas baubles, bells and bows. Remember that mistletoe and holly berries are toxic to humans, although a source of food for birds.

Carnivorous plant container

Venus fly trap (*Dionaea muscipula*), pitcher plants (*Nepenthes*), cobra lilies (*Darlingtonia californica*) and sundew (*Drosera*) are all suitable plants. Add moss to the container. Did you know that purple pitcher plant is the floral emblem of Newfoundland and Labrador in Canada?

Aquatic container

This container will be an excellent way to attract birds and insects to your garden area as they need to find water daily. Ideally, plant a mixture of floating and oxygenating plants such as water lilies (*Nymphaeaceae odorata*), arrowhead (*Sagittaria safittifolia*), sweet flag (*Acorus calamus*), water plantain (*Alisma*), water starworts (*Callitriche*) and water irises. Plants with submerged stems and leaves help provide food and shelter for water dwelling animals and provide a place for newt eggs to be hatched. No seaweed please as it's an algae and you will end up with 'pea soup'!

Zen or 'dry' landscape garden

A simple garden of stone and gravel (maybe with one specimen plant such as a cherry tree or maple), and a bowl of water represents a miniature version of our environment. For example, a large rock represents a mountain. There should be three zones: the foreground, the middle ground and the background. This is a garden for relaxation, meditation and imagination.

Alpine garden

Alpines are also known as rock plants which grow in a mountain climate. These plants like full sun and very good drainage. Use plants such as phlox, hens and chicks (also known as houseleeks or *Sempervivum*), pinks (*Dianthus*) and campanula.

Succulent garden

Succulents such as cacti originate from dry areas and are forced to store their own water. Not all succulents have spines and there are over 400 species to choose from. Ensure there is plenty of drainage in the container, such as gravel or stones, and that you use a good free draining potting mix. The succulent garden will thrive on neglect. Do not over water. Here are some suggestions that are easy to care for: sedum 'Autumn Joy', evergreen houseleeks (*Sempervivum* or hens and chicks), dwarf lewisia, rosularia and Parry's agave, which is a dwarf plant and very hardy.

Butterfly garden

This is a good idea if there is a teacher considering releasing butterflies at your school. As for the pollinator garden activity on p.80, try to have a variety of plants that bloom (with different size flowers from large to small) throughout the growing season. In particular butterflies seem to really like the colours purple and yellow. Each type of butterfly has a specific plant it prefers and they need different plants for different stages of their life. Here are some good plants to get started (some of which are herbs): bee balm, alyssum, day lilies, clover, parsley, sweet

William, lavender, mints, purple coneflower, sage, Shasta daisy, thistle, violet, nasturtium, marigold, stonecrop, phlox, yarrow and buddleia. Never use chemicals on your butterfly garden as it would poison butterfly larvae. The best fertilizers to improve the soil are garden compost and fish emulsions such as sea soil.

Vegetable garden container

Grow runner beans up a triangular trellis in the centre of a large container, with nasturtiums and cherry tomatoes around the edge.

Evergreen herb garden container

Plant a rosemary in the middle of the pot and plant around it herbs such as sage, santolina and thyme. You will be able to harvest from this container all year round.

Herb container with rosemary, purple sage, parsley (perennial) and oregano

Relaxation and Visualization Exercise for Deep Breathing

Before attempting this exercise with a group of children, make sure that the energy of the group of children is appropriate for this exercise specifically for it to be most effective. It may be a good idea to dig in the digging plot for ten minutes or to do another task in the garden before trying this visualization exercise.

Low muscle tone can affect breathing muscles, resulting in shallow breaths. Learning to breathe deeply helps us to stay calm and control respiration. If we can learn to self-control our impulses and aggressive tendencies through this visualization we are on the path to an improved standard of life and better able to deal with our peers.

If the moment is right and the sun is shining, take a few minutes to relax. A regular meditation's aim is to create awareness of self, to become more awake, but it is possible and perfectly acceptable to have a relaxation meditation.

If you are working with a child who is particularly anxious, this is an ideal exercise before starting a new activity. Allow ten minutes for this meditation and read the directions slowly, calmly and softly, with pauses in between to allow time for participants to process your words. Try to find a quiet setting to do this. Under a tree is a perfect setting. If there are loud noises or music is played nearby, it will be nearly impossible to focus on the relaxation exercise.

Sit comfortably and with your hands in your lap. You may sit on a chair or on the floor on a cushion as long as you are comfortable. You may keep your eyes open or close them.

Teacher/parent directions: speak the following words:

Relax.

Sit comfortably and try to let all your stress and tension fall away. Relax your shoulders.

Through sitting still quietly we can allow our mind to rest.

Breathe in and out slowly.

Become aware of how fast you are breathing. Relax.

Follow your breathing in and out. Breathing out through your nose. It may help to think of a white light emerging as your breath emerges out of the tip of your nose just like a dragon breathing.

Try not to let your mind wander. If it does, that is OK. Just try to focus on your breathing. In and out.

(pause here for two minutes)

You may be experiencing difficulty in focusing on the sensation of your breath. Relax.

Focus back on your breathing and the sensation you are experiencing. Try not to think about anything else. It's OK if your mind is wandering. It takes practice to focus on your breathing.

If your mind is wandering again return to the sensation of your breath.

(pause here for two minutes)

Slowly, you will begin to feel a sense of peace. Try to focus on these feelings.

(pause)

Use this meditation to develop good qualities to benefit yourself and for others.

Gradually, open your eyes, and have a stretch before you go on to another activity.

References

American Horticultural Therapy Association (AHTA) (2007) *Definitions and Positions*. AHTA Position Paper, available at www.abta.org/sitefiles/sitepages/c2c40f8e313a7002afab8d46beb97636.pdf (accessed 24 August 2011).

Armstrong, D. (2000) 'A community diabetes education and gardening project to improve diabetes care in a northwest American Indian tribe.' *Diabetes Educator 26*, 1, 113–120.

Barnicle, T. and Stoelzle Midden, K. (2003) 'The effects of a horticultural activity program on the psychological well-being of older people in a long-term care facility.' *HortTechnology 13*, 1, 81–85.

Blair, D., Giesecke, C. and Sherman, S. (1991) 'A dietary, social, and economic evaluation of the Philadelphia urban gardening project.' *Journal of Nutrition Education 23*, 161–167.

Bunn, D.E. (1986) 'Group cohesiveness is enhanced as children engage in plant stimulated discovery activities.' *Journal of Therapeutic Horticulture 1*, 37–43.

Cimprich, B. (1993) 'Development of an intervention to restore attention to cancer patients.' *Cancer Nursing 12*, 4, 22–27.

Cooper Marcus, C. and Barnes, M. (1999) *Healing gardens: Therapeutic benefits and design recommendations*. Chichester, UK: J. Wiley.

Csikszentmihalyi, M. (1990) *Flow: The Psychology of Optimal Experience*. New York: Harper and Row.

Feenstra, G., McGrew, S. and Campbell, D. (1999) *Entrepreneurial community gardens: Growing food, skills, jobs and communities*, Publication 21587. Davis, CA: University of California, Davis.

Friends Hospital (2005) *Healing with plants: The wonders of horticultural therapy*. www.friendshospitalonline.org/History.htm (accessed 22 October 2006).

Galindo, M. and Rodrieguez, J. (2000) 'Environmental aesthetics and psychological well-being: Relationships between preference judgements for urban landscapes and other relevant affective responses.' *Psychology in Spain 4*, 13–27.

Gerlach-Spriggs, N., Kaufman, R.E. and Warner, S.B. (1998) *Restorative gardens: The healing landscape*. New Haven, CT and London: Yale University Press.

Getzels, W. and Csikszentmihalyi, M. (1976) *The Creative Vision: A Longitudinal Study of Problem Finding in Art*. New York: Wiley.

Haller, R. and Kramer, C. (eds) (2006) *Horticultural therapy methods: Making connections in health care, human service, and community programs*. Binghamton, NY: The Haworth Press.

Hartig, T. (2003) 'Restorative environments: Guest editor's introduction.' *Environment and Behavior 33*, 4, 475–479.

Hartig, T., Mang, M. and Evans, G.W. (1991) 'Restorative effects of natural environment experiences.' *Environment and Behavior 23*, 1, 3–26.

Herzog, T., Black, A., Fountaine, K., Knotts, D. (1997) 'Reflection and attentional recovery as distinct benefits of restorative environments.' *Journal of Environmental Psychology 17*, 2, 165–170.

Hill, C. and Relf, P.D. (1982) 'Gardening as an outdoor activity in geriatric institutions.' *Activities, Adaptations and Aging 3*, 1, 47–54.

Jaffe, M.J. (1973) 'Thigmomorphogenesis: The response of plant growth and development to mechanical stimulation.' *Planta 114*, 2, 143–157.

Jarrott, S.E., Kwack, H.R. and Relf, D. (2002) 'An observational assessment of a dementia-specific horticultural therapy program.' *HortTechnology 12*, 3, 402–410.

Jellicoe, G. and Jellicoe, S. (1995) *Landscape of Man* (2nd ed.). London: Thames and Hudson.

Kaplan, R. (2001) 'The nature of the view from home: Psychological benefits.' *Environment and Behavior 33*, 4, 507–542.

Kaplan, R. and Kaplan, S. (1989) *The Experience of Nature*. New York: Cambridge University Press.

Kuo, F.E., Bacaicoa, M. and Sullivan, W.C. (1998) 'Transforming inner-city landscapes. Trees, sense of safety and preference.' *Environment and Behavior 30*, 1, 28–59.

Kweon, B.S., Sullivan, W.C. and Wiley, A.R. (1998) 'Green common spaces and the social integration of inner-city older adults.' *Environment and Behavior 30*, 6, 832–858.

Langer, E. and Rodin, J. (1976) 'The effects of choice and enhanced personal response for the aged: A field experiment in an institutional setting.' *Journal of Personality and Social Psychology 34*, 2, 191–198.

Louv, R. (2010) *The Nature Principle: Human Restoration and the End of Nature-Deficit Disorder*. Chapel Hill, NC: Algonquin.

Matsuo, E. (1995) 'Horticulture helps us to live as human beings: Providing balance and harmony in our behavior and thought and life worth living.' *Acta Horticulturae 391*, 19–30.

Mooney, P.F. and Milstein, S.L. (1994) 'Assessing the benefits of a therapeutic horticulture program for seniors in intermediate care.' In M. Francis, P. Lindsay and R.J. Stone (eds), *The Healing Dimension of People–Plant Relations: Proceedings of a Research Symposium* (pp.173–187). Davis, CA: University of California.

Moore, B. (1989) *Growing with Gardening: A Twelve-month Guide for Therapy, Recreation, and Education* (pp. 3-10). Chapel Hill, NC: University of North Carolina Press.

Namazi, K.H. and Haynes, S.R. (1994) 'Sensory stimuli reminiscence for patients with Alzheimer's disease: Relevance and implications.' *Clinical Gerontology 14*, 4, 29–45.

Perrins-Margalis, N., Rugletic, J., Schepis, N., Stepanski, H. and Walsh, M. (2000) 'The immediate effects of group-based horticulture on the quality of life of persons with chronic mental illness'. *Occupational Therapy in Mental Health 16*, 1, 15–30.

Pothukuchi, K. and Bickes, J. (2001) *Youth Nutrition Gardens in Detroit: A Report on Benefits, Potential, and Challenges*. Detroit, MI: Wayne State University.

Relf, P.D. (1978) 'Horticulture as a recreational activity.' *American Health Care Association Journal 4*, 5, 68–71.

Relf, P.D. (2006) 'Agriculture and Health Care: The Care of Plants and Animals for Therapy and Rehabilitation in the United States.' In J. Hassink and M. van Dijk (eds), *Farming for Health* (pp.309–343). The Netherlands: Springer.

Relf, D., McDaniel, A. and Butterfield, B. (1992) 'Attitudes toward plants and gardening.' *HortTechnology 2*, 201–204.

Rodiek, S. (2002) 'Influence of an outdoor garden on mood and stress in older persons.' *Journal of Therapeutic Horticulture 13*, 13–21.

Rush, B. (1812) *Medical inquiries and observations upon diseases of the mind*. Philadelphia, PA: Kimber & Richardson. Available at http://deila.dickinson.edu/theirownwords/title/0034.htm (accessed 22 October 2006).

Simson, S. and Straus, M. (1998) *Horticulture as Therapy: Principles and Practice*. Binghamton, NY: The Haworth Press.

Smith, D.V. and Aldous, D.E. (1994) 'Effect of Therapeutic Horticulture on the Self-concept of the Mildly Intellectually Disabled Student'. In M. Francis, P. Lindsay and R.J. Stone (eds), *The Healing Dimension of People–Plant Relations: Proceedings of a Research Symposium* (pp.215–221). Davis, CA: University of California.

Taylor, A.F., Kuo, F.E. and Sullivan, W.C. (2001) 'Coping with ADD: The surprising connection to green play settings.' *Environment and Behavior 33*, 54–77.

Ulrich, R.S. (1999) 'Effects of Gardens on Health Outcomes: Theory and Research.' In C. Cooper Marcus and M. Barnes (eds), *Healing Gardens: Therapeutic Benefits and Design Recommendations* (pp.27–86). New York: Wiley.

Ulrich, R.S. and Parsons, R. (1992) 'Influences of Passive Experiences with Plants on Individual Well-being and Health.' In D. Relf (ed), *The Role of Horticulture in Human Well-being and Social Development* (pp.93–105). Portland, OR: Timber Press.

Ulrich, R.S., Simons, R.F., Losito, B.D., Fiorito, E., Miles, M.A. and Zelson, M. (1991) 'Stress recovery during exposure to natural and urban environments.' *Journal of Environmental Psychology 11*, 201–230.

Vancouver Sun (2010) 'Soil bacterium may make us smarter.' 25 May.

Waliczek, T.M., Mattson, R.H. and Zajicek, J.M. (1996) 'Benefits of community gardening to quality of life issues.' *Journal of Environmental Horticulture 14*, 204–209.

Watson, D.P. and Burlingame, A.W. (1960) *Therapy through Horticulture*. New York: Macmillan.

Wells, N.M. (2000) 'At home with nature: Effects of "greenness" on children's cognitive functioning.' *Environment and Behavior 32*, 775–795.

Whitehouse, S., Varni, J.W., Seid, M., Cooper-Marcus, C., Ensberg, M.J., Jacobs, J.R. and Mehlenbeck, R.S. (2001) 'Evaluating a children's hospital garden environment: Utilization and consumer satisfaction.' *Journal of Environmental Psychology 21*, 301–314.

Wichrowski, M., Whiteson, J., Haas, F., Mola, A. and Rey, M. (2005) 'Effects of horticultural therapy on mood and heart rate in patients participating in an inpatient cardiopulmonary rehabilitation program.' *Journal of Cardiopulmonary Rehabilitation 25*, 5, 270–274.

Willets, H.C. and Sperling, A. (1983) *The Role of the Therapeutic Recreationist in Assisting the Oncology Patient to Cope*. New York: Futura.

Further Reading

Brickell, C. (1996) *The Royal Horticultural Society A–Z Encyclopedia of Garden Plants*. London: Dorling Kindersley.

Christopher, T. (2010) *The Green Hour*. Boston, MA: Trumpeter.

Hanh, T.N. (1975) *The Miracle of Mindfulness*. Boston, MA: Beacon.

Hewson, M.L. (1994) *Horticulture as Therapy*. Self-published by M. Hewson. Contact: hewsmitc@homewoodhealth.com

Kesseler, R. and Stuppy, W. (2006) *Seeds, Time Capsules of Life*. London: Papadakis.

Louv, R. (2008) *The Last Boy in the Woods: Saving Our Children from Nature-Deficit Disorder*. Chapel Hill, NC: Algonquin.

Louv, R. (2010) *The Nature Principle: Human Restoration and the End of Nature-Deficit Disorder*. Chapel Hill, NC: Algonquin.

Schoeberlein, D. (2009) *Mindful Teaching and Teaching Mindfulness*. Essex: Wisdom.

Simson, S. and Straus, M. (1998) *Horticulture as Therapy*. Pennsylvania, PA: Haworth.

Smith, D. and Search, G. (2004) *Delia's Kitchen Garden*. London: BBC Worldwide.

Titchmarsh, A. (2003) *How To Be a Gardener: Secrets of Success. Books One and Two*. London: BBC Worldwide.

Ward, J. (2008) *I Love Dirt!* Boston, MA: Trumpeter.

Yemm, H. (2010) *RHS Grow Your Own Flowers*. London: Octopus.

Recommended Resources

All websites were accessed 24 August 2011.

A. Wright & Son Ltd
www.penknives-and-scissors.co.uk
Manufacturer of fine quality pen and pocket knives.

American Horticultural Therapy Association (AHTA)
www.ahta.org
The AHTA advances the practice of horticulture as therapy to improve human well-being.

Ask Nature
www.asknature.org
This shows how scientists look at nature for solutions to everyday problems.

Canadian Horticultural Therapy Association (CHTA)
www.chta.ca
The Canadian Horticultural Therapy Association (CHTA) promotes the use of horticultural therapy and therapeutic horticulture for diverse populations and in a wide variety of settings.

Children and Nature Network (C&NN)
www.childrenandnature.org
C&NN is an international network dedicated to children's well-being and health through experiencing nature. Co-founded by Richard Louv.

Christopher and Dana Reeve Foundation
www.christopherreeve.org
The Reeve Foundation is dedicated to curing spinal cord injury by funding innovative research, and improving the quality of life for people living with paralysis through grants, information and advocacy.

Garden Organic
www.gardenorganic.org.uk
Formerly the Henry Doubleday Research Association (HDRA), Garden Organic is the UK's leading organic gardening organization. Its patron is HRH The Prince of Wales. Check out their free growing charts.

Geology for Kids
www.kidsgeo.com/geology-for-kids
A study of the earth and her people with a huge range of activities and games.

National Wildlife Federation (NWF)
www.greenhour.org
NWF launched GreenHour.org, an online resource providing parents with the inspiration and tools to make the outdoors a part of daily life.

Rick Hansen
www.rickhansen.com
Dedicated to improving the quality of life for people living with spinal cord injuries.

Royal Horticultural Society (RHS)
www.rhs.org.uk/schoolgardening
The RHS Campaign for School Gardening aims to encourage and support schools to create and actively use a school garden.

Science Kids
www.sciencekids.co.nz/projects.html
Science Kids educates children around the world on science and technology through experiments, activities and so on.

Soil Foodweb Canada
www.soilfoodweb.ca
Information about soil and other topics of interest to gardeners.

Thrive
www.thrive.org.uk
UK based charity that uses gardening to change lives.

Sources for adaptive tools

Disability Foundation
www.disabilityfoundation.org
The foundation promotes opportunities for people with disabilities. It provides many useful links to linked societies and information.

Lee Valley Tools
www.leevalley.com
International mail order and retail supplier for gardening and carpentry tools.

Peta (UK) Ltd
www.peta-uk.com
Designers, manufacturers and suppliers of ergonomic tools, aids and assistive devices for people suffering from arthritis or reduced grip strength.

Tetra Society of North America
www.tetrasociety.org
Dedicated to assisting people with disabilities to achieve an independent and fulfilling life through assistive devices.

Thrive: Carry on Gardening
www.carryongardening.org.uk
Practical information to make garden jobs easier, useful hints and tips and details of the equipment and tools which will be particularly helpful.

Information on toxic and non-toxic plants

British Columbia Drug and Poison Information Centre
www.dpic.org
For specific information see http://dpic.org/sites/default/files/pdf/PlantAwareness2007.pdf.

Washington Poison Center
www.wapc.org
A non-profit US organization with comprehensive lists of non-toxic and toxic plants.

Index